中国诗歌欣赏 Appreciation of Chinese Poetry

(第二版)

[美]王双双 编著

图书在版编目（CIP）数据

中国诗歌欣赏/（美）王双双编著. -- 2版. 北京：北京大学出版社，2024.6. --（新双双中文教材）. -- ISBN 978-7-301-35370-7

Ⅰ. H195.4

中国国家版本馆CIP数据核字第2024ME5752号

书　　　名	中国诗歌欣赏（第二版） ZHONGGUO SHIGE XINSHANG（DI-ER BAN）
著作责任者	[美]王双双　编著
英文翻译	张珴月
责任编辑	邓晓霞
英文校对	Arden Zhang
标准书号	ISBN 978-7-301-35370-7
出版发行	北京大学出版社
地　　　址	北京市海淀区成府路205号　100871
网　　　址	http://www.pup.cn　　新浪微博：@北京大学出版社
电子邮箱	zpup@pup.cn
电　　　话	邮购部 010-62752015　发行部 010-62750672　编辑部 010-62753334
印　刷　者	北京宏伟双华印刷有限公司
经　销　者	新华书店 889毫米×1194毫米　16开本　10.5印张　236千字 2007年3月第1版 2024年6月第2版　2024年6月第1次印刷
定　　　价	98.00元（含课本、练习本、音频）

未经许可，不得以任何方式复制或抄袭本书之部分或全部内容。
版权所有，侵权必究
举报电话：010-62752024　电子邮箱：fd@pup.cn
图书如有印装质量问题，请与出版部联系，电话：010-62756370

第二版序

能够与北京大学出版社合作出版"双双中文教材"的第二版，让这套优秀的对外汉语教材泽被更多的学生，加州中文教学研究中心倍感荣幸。

这是一套洋溢着浓浓爱意的教材。作者的女儿在美国出生，到了识字年龄，作者教她学习过市面上流行的多套中文教材，但都强烈地感觉到这些教材"水土不服"。一解女儿学习中文的燃眉之急，是作者编写这套教材的初衷和原动力。为了让没有中文环境的孩子能够喜欢学习中文，作者字斟句酌地编写课文；为了赋予孩子审美享受、引起他们的共鸣，作者特邀善画儿童创作了一幅幅稚气可爱的插图；为了加深孩子们对内容的理解，激发孩子们的学习热情，作者精心设计了充满创造性的互动活动。

这是一套承载着文化传承使命感的教材。语言不仅仅是文化的载体，更是文化重要的有机组成部分。学习一门外语的深层障碍往往根植于目标语言与母语间的文化差异。这种差异对于学习中文的西方学生尤为突出。这套教材的使用对象正处在好奇心和好胜心最强的年龄阶段，作者抓住了这一特点，变阻力为动力，一改过去削学生认知能力和智力水平之"足"以适词汇和语言知识之"履"的通病。教材在高年级部分，一个学期一个文化主题，以对博大精深的中国文化的探索激发学生的学习兴趣，使学生在学习语言的同时了解璀璨的中国文化。

"双双中文教材"自2005年面世以来，受到了老师、学生和家长的广泛欢迎。很多觉得中文学习枯燥无味而放弃的学生，因这套教材发现了学习中文的乐趣，又重新回到了中文课堂。本次修订，作者不仅吸纳了老师们对于初版的反馈意见和自己实际使用过程中的心得，还参考了近年对外汉语教学理论及实践方面的成果。语言学习部分由原来的九册改为五册，一学年学习一册，文化学习部分保持一个专题一册。相信修订后的"新双双中文教材"会更方便、实用，让更多学生受益。

张晓江

美国加州中文教学研究中心秘书长

第一版前言

"双双中文教材"是一套专门为海外青少年编写的中文课本,是我在美国八年的中文教学实践基础上编写而成的。在介绍这套教材之前,请读一首小诗:

> 一双神奇的手,
> 推开一扇窗。
> 一条神奇的路,
> 通向灿烂的中华文化。
>
> 鲍凯文　鲍维江

鲍维江和鲍凯文姐弟俩是美国生美国长的孩子,也是我的学生。1998年冬,他们送给我的新年贺卡上的小诗,深深地打动了我的心。我把这首诗看成我文化教学的"回声"。我要传达给海外每位中文老师:我教给他们(学生)中国文化,他们思考了、接受了、回应了。这条路走通了!

语言是一种交流的工具,更是一种文化和一种生活方式,所以学习中文也就离不开中华文化的学习。汉字是一种古老的象形文字,她从远古走来,带有大量的文化信息,但学起来并不容易。使学生增强兴趣、减小难度,走出苦学汉字的怪圈,走进领悟中华文化的花园,是我编写这套教材的初衷。

学生不论大小,天生都有求知的欲望,都有欣赏文化美的追求。中华文化本身是魅力十足的。把这宏大而玄妙的文化,深入浅出地、有声有色地介绍出来,让这迷人的文化如涓涓细流,一点一滴地渗入学生们的心田,使学生们逐步体味中国文化,是我编写这套教材的目的。

为此我将汉字的学习放入文化介绍的流程之中同步进行,让同学们在学中国地理的同时,学习汉字;在学中国历史的同时,学习汉字;在学中国哲学的同时,学习汉字;在学中国科普文选的同时,学习汉字……

这样的一种中文学习,知识性强,趣味性强;老师易教,学生易学。当学生们合上书本时,他们的眼前是中国的大好河山,是中国五千年的历史和妙不可言的哲学思维,是奔腾的现代中国……

总之,他们了解了中华文化,就会探索这片土地,热爱这片土地,就会与中国结下情缘。

最后我要衷心地感谢所有热情支持和帮助我编写教材的老师、家长、学生、朋友和家人。特别是老同学唐玲教授、何茜老师和我女儿Uta Guo年复一年的鼎力相助。可以说这套教材是大家努力的结果。

王双双

课程设置（建议）

序号	书名	适用年级
1	中文课本　第一册	幼儿园/一年级
2	中文课本　第二册	二年级
3	中文课本　第三册	三年级
4	中文课本　第四册	四年级
5	中文课本　第五册	五年级
6	中国成语故事	六年级
7	中国地理常识	
8	中国古代故事	七年级
9	中国神话传说	
10	中国古代科学技术	八年级
11	中国民俗与民间艺术	
12	中国文学欣赏	九年级
13	中国诗歌欣赏	
14	中国古代哲学	十年级
15	中国历史	

目录

第一课　诗经 …………………………………… 1

第二课　屈原与楚辞 …………………………… 9

第三课　乐府 …………………………………… 16

第四课　唐诗（一） …………………………… 28

第五课　唐诗（二） …………………………… 40

第六课　宋词（一） …………………………… 47

第七课　宋词（二） …………………………… 54

第八课　宋词（三） …………………………… 65

第九课　古诗词二首 …………………………… 74

第十课　现代诗 ………………………………… 83

生字表（简） …………………………………… 91

生字表（繁） …………………………………… 92

生词表（简） …………………………………… 93

生詞表（繁） …………………………………… 95

第一课

诗经

《诗经》是中国第一部诗歌总集,共305篇,相传由孔子所编。当我们打开《诗经》时,读到的是2500—3000年前的诗歌,古老优美的诗句讲述了爱情、婚礼、劳动、宴会、战争等,还讲述了山川鸟兽等自然风貌,内容十分丰富。《诗经》也是中国古代诗歌的起点,对后世的诗歌影响深远。

关 雎(节选)

关关雎鸠,在河之洲。
窈窕淑女,君子好(hǎo)逑。

【注释】

关关:鸟的叫声。
雎鸠:一种水鸟。
逑(ǒu):配偶。

【讲解】

"关雎"是《诗经》中的第一篇,一首爱情诗。

水鸟关关对着唱,相伴河中沙洲上。
美丽善良好姑娘,君子追求的好对象。

采　葛

彼采葛兮,一日不见,如三月兮!
彼采萧兮,一日不见,如三秋兮!
彼采艾兮,一日不见,如三岁兮!

【注释】

葛:植物名,花紫红色,根可作药用。

彼:那、那个;对方、他。

兮:助词,跟现代文的"啊"相似。

萧:植物名,即青蒿,有香气。

艾:植物名,叶子有香气,可用作药材。

【讲解】

那个采葛的姑娘啊,一天没有见到她,就像隔了三个月呀!

那个采萧的姑娘啊,一天没有见到她,就像隔了三个秋季那样长啊!

那个采艾的姑娘啊,一天没有见到她,就像隔了三年那样长又长呀!

这首诗短短几句,表现了对情人越来越思念的心情。至今人们仍然用"一日不见,如隔三秋"来形容强烈的思念。

王金泰　画

一日不见,如隔三秋

生词

zǒng jí 总集	collection		shū nǚ 淑女	lady
jiǎng shù 讲述	tell about		qiú 逑	mate
yàn huì 宴会	feast, banquet		bǐ 彼	that; she; he
fēng mào 风貌	style and features		xī 兮	*auxiliary word*
jū jiū 雎鸠	osprey		xiāo 萧	mugwort
yǎo tiǎo 窈窕	slim		ài 艾	mugwort

听写

总集　讲述　宴会　风貌　彼　兮

背诵并默写

《关雎》

比一比

集 { 总集 / 集体 }　　述 { 讲述 / 述说 }　　影 { 电影 / 影响 }

| 编 |　　| 篇 |

编写　　　一篇文章

词语运用

影响

① 玩电子游戏太多，会影响学习。

② 家庭环境会影响人的成长。

③ 疫情影响了人们的正常生活。

词语解释

后世——后来的时代。

君子——有学问有修养，品德好的人，这里指男青年。

资料

《诗经》

《诗经》是中国第一部诗歌总集，书中记录了西周初年至春秋时期约五六百年间的各种诗歌。这些诗歌许多来自民间。周代专门设置了采诗官，到各地收集民间歌谣，借以向天子反映百姓的生活。也有一些诗歌来自文人创作，反映了政治和贵族生活等。《诗经》为我们讲述了两千多年以前的中国样貌，如天文地理、民间风俗等方方面面。

Lesson One

The Book of Songs

The Book of Songs is the first collection of poems in China, consisting of 305 poems in total. It is said to have been compiled by Confucius. In *The Book of Songs* we encounter a diverse collection of poems that date back to 2500 to 3000 years, with the ancient and beautiful verses narrating various themes such as love, weddings, agricultural labor, feasts, wars, and the natural world including mountains, forests, birds, and animals. *The Book of Songs* also marks the beginning of ancient Chinese poetry and has had a profound influence on poetry in later periods.

Guan Ju (excerpt)

Guan Guan,
The ospreys sing,
On the river islet perching.
The elegant and virtuous maiden,
Is the perfect match for the noble young man.

[Annotation]
关关：the sound of birds calling
雎鸠：a type of waterfowl
好：mutual attraction between men and women
逑：spouse or partner

[Explanation of the Poem]
"Guan Ju," a love poem, is the first poem in *The Book of Songs*.

Waterbirds call and accompany each other on the sandbanks of the river.
The beautiful and virtuous young lady is the ideal match for the noble gentlemen.

Picking Arrowroot

To pick the arrowroot she is gone.
One day without seeing her feels like three months long!
To pick the common fern she is gone.
One day without seeing her feels like three autumns long!
To pick the mug wort she is gone.
One day without seeing him feels like three years long!

[Annotation]

葛: arrowroot. a plant with purple-red flowers. Its root can be used as medicine.

彼: that, that one, he or she.

兮: a particle functioning similarly with "ah" in modern language.

萧: mug wort. a plant with a fragrant aroma, also known as common fern.

艾: worm wood. a plant with aromatic leaves, often used for medicinal purposes.

[Explanation of the Poem]

She is gone to pick the arrowroot.
A day without seeing her feels like three months.
She is gone to pick the common fern.
A day without seeing her feels like three autumns.
She is gone to pick the mug wort.
A day without seeing her feels like three years.

This short poem, consisting of only a few lines, expresses the growing longing for a lover. Even today, people still use "a day without seeing you feels like three autumns" to describe intense feelings of longing.

Data

The Book of Songs is the first comprehensive collection of poetry in China. The book contains various poems from the early Western Zhou period to the Spring and Autumn period, spanning approximately five to six centuries. Many of these poems originated from the common people. During the Zhou Dynasty, a position called "the Collector of Poems" was established to collect folk songs from different regions, with the purpose of reflecting the lives of the people to the emperor. Some other poems in the collection were composed by aristocrats and literati, focusing primarily on narrative and the portrayal of customs. *The Book of Songs* provides us with insights into China over several thousand years ago, covering varies aspects such as astronomy, geography, and folk customs.

第二课

屈原与楚辞

屈原（约前340—约前278）是战国时期楚国人，中国历史上第一位伟大的诗人。他创造了一种新的诗歌形式——楚辞。楚辞与《诗经》是中国诗歌的源头。

楚辞是在南方浪漫民风的影响下，在民歌的基础上发展起来的，诗句为自由的长短句。句中、句尾常用"兮"字表示语气。楚辞诗体新鲜，表现力强。

屈原一生写出了许多优秀的诗歌，其中最著名的是《离骚^{sāo}》。在《离骚》中，他写出了自己不幸的一生和被放逐后的悲愤，以及

王金泰　画

对楚国人民的热爱之情。如：

路漫漫其修远兮，（我要走的路是多么漫长啊，）

吾将上下而求索。（我将上天入地去追求理想。）

《离骚》感情奔放，语句美丽动人。

楚辞的产生与屈原苦难的一生是分不开的。屈原是楚国人。楚国在长江流域，是一个有五千里山河的大国。屈原早年受楚怀王重用，做过高官。他主张联合其他国家共同抵抗秦国。没想到，楚怀王不但没有采用他的主张，反而把他赶出国都。屈原在后来的放逐生活中，一直关心着楚国的命运。看到热爱的楚国越来越弱，一次次被秦军打败，他悲痛万分，写出了《离骚》《天问》等诗歌。屈原头发散乱，面容黄瘦，一边走一边唱着伤心的歌。有人劝他到别的国家去，他说"鸟飞累了想回到自己的老枝上歇息；狐狸死了，头还向着土山，我不能离开楚国"。最后，秦军攻破了楚国的都城，屈原的心碎了，在农历五月初五投江自杀。

相传，老百姓听说屈原投江以后，马上划船去救他，可是没有找到。因为怕他的尸体被鱼吃掉，人们往江里撒米喂鱼。从此以后，人们为了纪念屈原，每年农历五月初五都要赛龙舟、吃粽子，过端午节。

第二课

生 词

qū yuán 屈原	name of a poet	lián hé 联合	unite
chǔ cí 楚辞	*a style of a poem, a poetic form*	dǐ kàng 抵抗	resist
xíng shì 形式	form	mìng yùn 命运	destiny, fate
làng màn 浪漫	romantic	xiē 歇	rest
jī chǔ 基础	basis, foundation	shī tǐ 尸体	dead body, corpse
fàng zhú 放逐	banish; exile	sǎ 撒	scatter
bēi fèn 悲愤	grief and indignation	zòng zi 粽子	*a food made of glutinous rice wrapped in bamboo leaves*
qiú suǒ 求索	seek		
bēn fàng 奔放	uninhibited	duān wǔ jié 端午节	Dragon Boat Festival

听 写

屈原　楚辞　形式　浪漫　基础　联合　抵抗　歇

尸体　端午节　悲愤　*粽子

注：*以后的字词为选做题，后同。

11

背诵并默写

路漫漫其修远兮，吾将上下而求索。

比一比

基 { 基础 / 基本 }　　　漫 { 浪漫 / 漫长 }　　　形 { 形式 / 形狀 }

词语运用

浪漫

① 《牛郎织女》是一个浪漫的民间故事。

② 他们过了一个浪漫的情人节。

漫长

① 中国北方的冬季十分漫长。

② 在她漫长的一生中，遇到过许多困难。

词语解释

源头——意思是水发源处，比喻事物的本源。

路漫漫——路又远又长。

阅读

端午节纪念屈原

- 端午节在每年农历五月初五
- 为纪念伟大的爱国诗人屈原
- 人们吃粽子,举办赛龙舟活动

崔建岐　画

Lesson Two

Qu Yuan and *Chu Ci*

Qu Yuan (approximately 340 BC–278 BC) was a native of the State of Chu during the Warring States period. He is regarded as the first great poet in Chinese history. He pioneered a new form of poetry called "Chu Ci" which together with *The Book of Songs* are the origins of Chinese poetry.

With its foundation being folk songs, *Chu Ci* developed under the influence of the romantic folk culture in the southern regions. Its poetry features free verse, using both long and short lines. The particle "兮" is often used within sentences and at the end of sentences to convey a particular tone. *Chu Ci* poetry is known for its freshness and strong expressive power.

Being one famous poet of *Chu Ci*, Qu Yuan wrote many outstanding poems throughout his life, with the most famous being "Li Sao" （离骚）.

In "Li Sao" Qu Yuan expressed the unfortunate events of his life, his bitterness after being exiled, and his deep love for the people of the State of Chu. For example:

"The road stretches long and far, oh, how long it is, I will search high and low, up and down, in pursuit of my ideals."

Li Sao is passionate in its emotions, beautiful and moving in its diction.

The creation of *Chu Ci* is closely tied to the hardships in Qu Yuan's life. Qu Yuan was from the State of Chu, located in the Yangtze River basin, a vast nation with five thousand li of mountains and rivers. In his early years, Qu Yuan held a high position in the government under King Huai of Chu. He advocated for uniting with other states to resist the Qin state. However, King Huai not only rejected his advice but also exiled him from the capital city. Throughout his life in exile, Qu Yuan continued to care about the fate of the State of Chu. Seeing the country he loved weakening and repeatedly defeated by the Qin army, he became saddened and wrote poems like "Li Sao" and "Tian Wen." Qu Yuan's hair became disheveled, his face became thin and pale, and he sang mournful songs as he wandered. Some people advised him to go to other countries, but he said, "When a bird is tired, it wants to return to its old branch for rest; when a fox dies, its head still points toward the native soil. I can't leave the State of Chu." In the end, the Qin army captured the capital of Chu, and Qu Yuan's heart was broken. On the fifth day of the fifth lunar month, he threw himself into the river and ended his life.

According to legend, as soon as the common people heard that Qu Yuan had jumped into the river, they rowed boats in a rush to rescue him but couldn't retrieve his body. Fearing that his corpse would be eaten by fish, people scattered rice into the river to feed the fish. Since then, in commemoration of Qu Yuan, every year on the fifth day of the fifth lunar month, people race dragon boats and eat zongzi to celebrate the Dragon Boat Festival.

Commemorating Qu Yuan on the Dragon Boat Festival

✧ The Dragon Boat Festival falls on the fifth day of the fifth lunar month each year.

✧ It is observed to commemorate the great patriotic poet, Qu Yuan.

✧ During the Dragon Boat Festival, people eat zongzi and partake in the activity of dragon boat racing.

第三课

乐府

"乐府"最初是管理音乐的机构，始于秦代。汉代，乐府负责从民间收集诗歌，收集到的诗歌叫"乐府民歌"。这些诗歌语言朴素生动，内容广泛。代表作有南北朝时期的《木兰辞[①]》。后来，人们把"乐府"作为一种诗体，创作了很多乐府诗。

木兰辞（节选）

唧(jī)唧复唧唧，木兰当户织。不闻机杼(zhù)声，唯闻女叹息。

问女何所思？问女何所忆？女亦无所思，女亦无所忆。

昨夜见军帖，可汗(kè hán)大点兵。军书十二卷，卷卷有爷名。

阿爷无大儿，木兰无长兄，愿为市鞍(ān)马，从此替爷征。

东市买骏马，西市买鞍鞯(jiān)，南市买辔(pèi)头，北市买长鞭。

朝辞爷娘去，暮宿黄河边。

不闻爷娘唤女声，但闻黄河流水鸣溅溅(jiān)。

万里赴戎(róng)机，关山度若飞。

[①] 辞——中国古代一种文体。

将军百战死,壮士十年归。

归来见天子,天子坐明堂。

可汗问所欲, 木兰不用尚书郎,

愿驰千里足,送儿还故乡。

爷娘闻女来,出郭相扶将。

小弟闻姊(zǐ)来,磨刀霍霍(huò)向猪羊。

开我东阁门,坐我西阁床。脱我战时袍,著我旧时裳。

当窗理云鬓(bìn),对镜帖花黄。出门看火伴,火伴皆惊忙。

同行十二年,不知木兰是女郎。

王宜珈　画

【注释】

唧唧：叹息声。

机杼：机，指织布机。杼（suō），织布机的梭子。

可汗：古代西北民族对君主的称呼。

市鞍马：市，买。鞍马，泛指马和马具。

鞍鞯：马鞍和马鞍下面的垫子（diàn）。

辔头：马嚼子（jiáo）、笼头和缰绳（jiāng）。

赴戎机：奔赴战场。戎机：指战争。

关山度若飞：像飞一样越过一道道的关，一座座的山。度，越过。

不用尚书郎：不用，不愿意做。尚书，古代高官的名称。

郭：外城。

霍霍：磨刀的声音。

著：读zhuó，穿。

裳：这里读作cháng，古音，指下衣。

火伴：古代军队十人为一火，同灶吃饭。现泛指共同参加某种组织或活动的人，写作伙伴。

【讲解】

唧唧，唧唧，木兰在门前织布，听不见织布的声音，只听见她在叹息。问木兰："你在想什么，在思念什么呢？"木兰说没有想什么，也没有思念什么。"昨天晚上看见征兵的文书，可汗在大征兵，征兵的名册有父亲的名字。"父亲没有成年的儿子，木兰没有兄长，木兰决定去买鞍买马，替父亲出征。

木兰在集市买了骏马、鞍子等，一早辞别父母上路，晚上到了黄河边，听不见父母呼唤女儿的声音，只听到黄河水流的声音。万里奔赴战场，像飞一样地跨过一道道关山。将士们出生入死地战斗，多年后活着的人才回来。木兰胜利归来进见天子，天子坐在明亮的殿堂上。问木兰有什么要求。木兰说不愿做大官，只想骑上一匹千里马返回故乡。

木兰父母听说女儿回来，互相扶持着出城去迎接；小弟听说木兰回来，把刀磨得亮亮的去杀猪宰羊。回到家木兰打开房间东边的门，坐在房间西边的床上，脱下战袍，穿上以前的衣裙，坐在窗前对着镜子整理头发，还在额头上贴上漂亮的花片。当她出门去见伙伴，伙伴们都惊呆了：一同出征这么多年，都不知道木兰是女孩呢。

生 词

乐府 yuè fǔ	Yue Fu	暮 mù	twilight
朴素 pǔ sù	plain	唤 huàn	call out
广泛 guǎng fàn	extensive	赴 fù	go to
亦 yì	either, too	欲 yù	want
军帖 jūn tiě	military announcement	阁 gé	boudoir
替 tì	for	裳 cháng	clothing, attire
征 zhēng	go out to battle	皆 jiē	both
骏马 jùn mǎ	fine horse		

听写

乐府　朴素　广泛　替　征　骏马　赴　欲

伙伴　皆　*衣裳　暮

背诵

《木兰辞》"唧唧复唧唧"到"从此替爷征"。

比一比

忆 { 回忆 / 记忆 }　　辞 { 告辞 / 辞别 }　　帖 { 军帖 / 请帖 }

朝	暮
早晨	傍晚

词语运用

朴素

① 爷爷一直在农村，生活简单朴素。

② 姐姐喜欢米色的衣服，很朴素。

广泛

① 《木兰辞》是一首在中国民间广泛流传的诗歌。

② 手机现在被人们广泛使用。

多音字

zhāo
朝

朝阳

cháo
朝

汉朝

反义词

朝——暮　　　归来——离去

词语解释

民歌——民间口头流传的歌曲。

姊—— 姐姐。

游子吟

[唐]孟郊

慈母手中线,游子身上衣。

临行密密缝,意恐迟迟归。

谁言寸草心,报得三春晖(huī)。

王金泰 画

【注释】

临行：临走前。

意：心愿，心意。

迟：慢，晚。

晖：阳光。

【讲解】

这是一首乐府诗，描写了慈爱的母亲为远行的儿子细针密线地缝衣服，生怕儿子一去几年迟迟不归。谁说小草能报答春日的阳光，儿女又怎能报答母亲的恩(ēn)情！诗歌真切地述说母爱，千百年来打动着每一位读者。

生词

吟 (yín)	chant; sing	慈母 (cí mǔ)	loving mother
郊 (jiāo)	suburb		

背诵

《游子吟》

作者简介

孟郊（751—814），唐代诗人。这首诗是他当了官后，回家去接母亲时所作。

Lesson Three

Yue Fu

First established during the Qin Dynasty, Yue Fu is the official institution responsible for managing music. During the Han Dynasty, Yue Fu oversaw collecting poems from the common people, and the collected poems were referred to as "Yue Fu folk songs." These poems were written in simple and vivid language and covered a wide range of topics. A famous example is the poem *the Ballad of Mulan* from the Southern and Northern Dynasties period. Later, poets used "Yue Fu" as a poetic form and created many poems in this style.

The Ballad of Mulan (Excerpt)

Jiji, jiji, by the door Mulan is weaving.
No sound of loom or shuttle is heard but only her sighing.
"Girl, what is on your mind?
what are you missing?"
"I think of nothing, and nothing am I missing.
Last night, Mulan saw the military order;
The Khan is drafting a big army.
The military order runs twelve scrolls long,
Father's name is in everyone.
Father has no elder son;
Elder brother Mulan has none.
Mulan is willing to buy a horse and saddle in the market,
In Father's place she will fight."

Buy a fine horse in the east market;
Buy a saddle and the cushion under the saddle in the west market.
Buy a bridle in the south market;
Buy a long whip in the north market.

Farewell to father and mother in the morning,
Arriving at the Yellow River in the evening.
Hear not parents' voices calling her,

But only the splashing of the Yellow River.
Traveling thousands of li to the battlefield,
Cross mountains like flying.

The general perishes after a hundred battles;
After ten years the valiant warriors return.

Upon returning, Mulan sees the Son of Heaven,
The Son of Heaven sits in the bright hall.
The Khan asks Mulan what she desires,
"Mulan does not seek an official position,
I only wish to borrow a swift horse to go back to my hometown."

When her parents hear that their daughter is returning,
They come out to the gate to meet her.
Her younger brother hears of his sister's return,
He sharpens the knife to slaughter pigs and sheep to treat her.

Open my east chamber door;
Sit on my west chamber bed.
Take off my armor from the battlefield;
Put on my old-time attire.

By the window, arrange my cloudy hair,
In front of the mirror, attach yellow blossoms to the forehead.

She goes out and looks at her comrades;
The comrades are all in shock.
During the twelve years of companionship,
They had never known Mulan was a woman.

[Annotation]

唧唧：the chirping sound of insects

机杼：a shuttle used in weaving

可汗：a title used by ancient Northwest People for a king or ruler

市鞍马："市" means to buy or trade, and "鞍马" refers to horses and their equipment.

鞍鞯：refers to the saddle and the cushion under the saddle

辔头：the bit and reins used for controlling a horse

赴戎机：to rush to the battlefield. "戎机" refers to warfare.

关山度若飞：crossing overpasses and mountains as if flying. "度" means to cross over.

不用尚书郎："不用" refers to not wanting to, and "尚书" was a title for high-ranking officials

in ancient times.

郭：outside the city

霍霍：the sound of sharpening a knife

著：pronounced as zhuó, it means to put on or wear.

裳：in this context, pronounced as cháng, it refers to a skirt or clothing.

火伴：in ancient times, ten soldiers were grouped together as a fire unit and shared a cooking pot. Nowadays, the term "fire" is used more broadly to refer to people who participate in the same organization or activity, often written as "companion."

[Explanation of the Poem]

The insects are chirping, and Mulan is weaving in front of her door. You can't hear the sound of weaving; you only hear her sighing.

They ask Mulan, "What are you thinking? What are you longing for?"

Mulan says she's not thinking about anything, not longing for anything.

"Last night I saw the conscription notice. The Khan is conscripting soldiers, and on the conscription list, I saw my father's name." Her father has no grown sons, and Mulan has no elder brothers, so what can be done? Mulan decides to buy a saddle and a horse and go to the army on her father's behalf.

Mulan goes to the market and buys a fine horse, saddle, and so on. Early the next day, she bids farewell to her parents and sets out. At night, she stops by the Yellow River and stays there. She can't hear her parents calling for her; she only hears the sound of the Yellow River flowing. She rushes to the battlefield, crossing mountain passes as if flying. The soldiers fight and sacrifice, and many years later, the survivors return. Mulan returns victorious and meets the emperor. The emperor sits in a bright hall and asks Mulan if she has any requests. Mulan says she doesn't want high office; she only wants a fast horse to return to her hometown.

Mulan's parents hear that their daughter has returned, and they go out of the city to welcome her, supporting each other. Mulan's younger brother hears that she's back, and he sharpens his knife to slaughter pigs and sheep. Back at home, Mulan opens the east gate of the room, sits on the bed of the west, takes off her armor, puts on her old clothes, sits in front of the mirror to tidy her hair, and even places a beautiful flower on her forehead. When she goes out to meet her comrades, they are all astonished: after all these years of going to war together, they never knew Mulan was a girl.

Song of the Departing Son

By Meng Jiao, Tang Dynasty

The thread in the hand of my loving mother,

Weaves out the clothes for me.

Before my departure she stitches it closely,

Fearing I might return home late.

Who says that the gratitude of the inch-long grass,

Can repay the warm spring sun rays?

[Annotation]

临行：before departing

意：desire, intention

迟：slow, late

晖：sunshine, radiance, same as "辉"

[Explanation of the Poem]

This is a poem written in the Yue Fu style that depicts a loving mother sewing clothes with a fine needle and close stitches for her son going on a long journey. She is afraid that her son will be away for long time before returning. Just as it's said that the little grass can't repay the spring sunlight, how can children ever repay the kindness and love of their mother? This poem vividly conveys the depth of a mother's love and has touched the heart of readers for thousands of years.

[Author's Biography]

Meng Jiao (751-814) was a renowned poet of the Tang Dynasty in China. He wrote this poem upon returning home to meet his mother after assuming an official position.

第四课

唐诗（一）

唐代的诗歌，是中国古代诗歌的高峰，那时诗人多，诗歌也多。诗歌中律诗和绝句很盛行。律诗八句，每句五字的，称五言律诗；每句七字的，称七言律诗。绝句四句，每句五字的，称五言绝句；每句七字的，称七言绝句。律诗和绝句要求声律和对仗，读起来十分动听。唐代最著名的诗人有李白、杜甫(fǔ)和白居易等。

登鹳(guàn)雀楼
（五言绝句）

［唐］王之涣(huàn)

白日依山尽，

黄河入海流。

欲穷千里目，

更上一层楼。

王金泰　画

【注释】

鹳雀楼：在山西省永济市，位于黄河边，是唐代的名胜。

依：依傍，紧挨(āi)着。

尽：完，到头，这里指太阳落山。

欲：想要。

穷：用尽。

更：再。

【讲解】

诗的前两句描写作者从鹳雀楼远望的壮观景象：傍晚，太阳在起伏的群山中慢慢落下，滚滚的黄河水向远方奔流而去。这高山大河的壮美画面，令诗人感叹。随着一步步登上楼的高层，诗人的视线越来越远，眼界越来越开阔。这使人感悟到一个哲理：只有站得更高，才能看得更远。

望庐山瀑布
（七言绝句）

［唐］李白

日照香炉生紫烟，
遥看瀑布挂前川。
飞流直下三千尺，
疑是银河落九天。

王金泰　画

【注释】

庐山：中国名山，在江西省。

香炉：指庐山的香炉峰。

九天：指天，"九"字形容天高到极点。

【讲解】

　　作者用夸张的手法写出了庐山瀑布的壮丽景色：阳光照着香炉峰，紫云袅(niǎo)袅。从远处看去，瀑布高高地挂在石壁上。瀑布从高山顶上飞流直下，就好像是九重天上的银河落了下来。

生词

lǜ shī 律诗	regulated verse	lú shān 庐山	Lushan Mountain
jué jù 绝句	quatrain	pù bù 瀑布	waterfall
yán 言	word, character		

背诵并默写

《登鹳雀楼》和《望庐山瀑布》

比一比

瀑（瀑布）
爆（爆炸）

层 { 一层
     地层

律 { 律师
     律诗

词语解释

声律——语言的声调韵律。"声"指声调,"律"指韵律。

对仗——是把同类或表示对立概念的词语放在对应的位置上,起到相互衬托的作用。

春夜喜雨
（五言律诗）

［唐］杜甫

好雨知时节，当春乃发生。

随风潜入夜，润物细无声。

野径云俱黑，江船火独明。

晓看红湿处，花重锦官城。

【注释】

知：明白，知道。

乃发生：乃，就；发生，出现。

潜：悄悄地。

润物：（雨水）滋养万物。

野径：田野间的小路。

俱：全、都，与下句"独"字相对。

红湿处：沾满雨水的花朵。红，指花朵；湿，指沾满雨水。

锦官城：成都的别称。

【讲解】

好雨知道节气，在春天植物发芽时下起来了。

春雨随风在夜里悄悄落下，静静滋润着万物。

村野小路和乌云一片漆黑，只有江船上灯火明亮。

清晨再看满城的花朵，都带着雨水沉甸甸的。

诗人满心欢喜地描写了及时到来的春雨和成都夜雨的景象。

生 词

乃 nǎi just

潜入 qián rù quietly infiltrate

锦 jǐn brocade

阅读

声律启蒙 《笠(qǐ)翁(lì wēng)对韵》（节选）

云对雨，雪对风，

晚照对晴空。

来鸿对去燕，宿鸟对鸣虫。

三尺剑，六钧(jūn)弓，

北岭(lǐng)对江东。

人间清暑殿，天上广寒宫。

两岸晓烟杨柳绿，

一园春雨杏花红。

崔建岐　画

《笠翁对韵》介绍

《笠翁对韵》由明末清初文学家李渔创作，是一本声律启蒙的读物。

Lesson Four

Poetry in Tang Dynasty (I)

Chinese ancient poetry reached its pinnacle in the Tang Dynasty when poets and poetry thrived. Within the realm of poetry, regulated verse (律诗, lǜshī) and quatrains (绝句, juéjù) were prevalent.

Regulated verse typically consists of eight lines, each containing five characters, known as "five-character regulated verse." There were also seven-character-regulated verses with seven characters per line. Quatrains, on the other hand, usually have four lines. Each line either contains five characters, referred to as "five-character quatrains" or seven characters, called "seven-character quatrains." Both regulated verse and quatrains require adherence to tonal and rhyme patterns, making them sound very melodious when read aloud. Some of the most famous poets of the Tang Dynasty include Li Bai, Du Fu, and Bai Juyi, among others.

Atop the Stork Tower
(Five-Character Quatrains)
By Wang Zhihuan, Tang Dynasty

The white sun beside the hill glows,
The Yellow River to the sea flows.
To enjoy a grander sight,
I climb a greater height.

[Annotation]

鹳雀楼：Stork Tower. Located in Yongji City, Shanxi Province, it stands by the side of the Yellow River and is a famous scenic spot from the Tang Dynasty.

依：to lean or be close to

尽：to complete or reach the end. Here, it refers to the setting of the sun

欲：to want or desire

穷：to exhaust or use up

更：again or furthermore

[Explanation of the Poem]

The first two lines of the poem describe the magnificent scene that the author sees from Stork Tower: At twilight the sun slowly sets behind the rolling mountains; the rushing waters of the Yellow

River flow to the distant sea. The poet is in awe of the grand and beautiful view of these towering mountains and the mighty river. As he climbs the tower step by step, his view becomes broader, and his perspective widens, leading him to realize a profound truth: Only by standing higher can one see farther.

Viewing the Waterfall at Lushan Mountain
(Seven-Character Quatrains)
By Li Bai, Tang Dynasty

Purple mist arises from the sunlit Incense-Burner Peak,
In the distance I see the waterfall hangs over the hill in front of me.
Straightly down like flying from three thousand feet high the torrent rushes,
I wonder if it is the Milky Way falling from Heaven Ninth.

[Annotation]

庐山：a famous mountain in China located in Jiangxi Province.

香炉：refers to the Xianglu Peak of Lushan Mountain.

九天：refers to the heaven or sky. The number "nine" means it's the highest point in the sky.

[Poem Explanation]

The author employs a poetic exaggeration to vividly depict the magnificent scene of the Lushan Mountain waterfall: In the early morning, as the sunlight illuminates Incense-Burner Peak, purplish mists evaporate from the waterfall. When viewed from a distance, the waterfall appears to hang high on the cliff. The waterfall descends rapidly from the mountaintop, resembling nothing less than the Milky Way cascading down from the heavens above.

[Diction Explanation]

声律：tonal and rhyme patterns. "声" refers to the tones of the characters, while "律" pertains to the rhythmic patterns and rhymes in the language. In Chinese poetry, maintaining specific tonal and rhythmic patterns is crucial for creating a harmonious and melodious composition.

对仗：parallelism. It is a technique in Chinese poetry where words or phrases with similar or contrasting meanings are placed in corresponding positions within the lines. This technique adds balance, symmetry, and contrast to the poem, enhancing its aesthetic and rhetorical effects.

[Selective]

Happy Rain on a Spring Night

(Five-Character Regulated Verse)

By Du Fu, Tang Dynasty

A good rain knows the season right,
In spring it falls just in time.
With the wind it creeps into the night,
Moistening everything soft and quiet.
Over wild lanes dark clouds spread,
In the river boat a lantern looms.
Dawn sees flowers wet and red,
The city of Chengdu is heavy with blooms.

[Annotation]

知：to know, to understand

乃发生："乃" refers to just, and "发生" means to happen.

潜：quietly

润物：nourishing all living things with rainwater

野径：rural paths

俱：all, collectively. Contrasting with the next word "独".

红湿处：the places where flowers are moistened by rainwater. "红" refers to flowers, and "湿" means wet or soaked, particularly with rainwater.

锦官城：An alternative name for Chengdu, known for its splendid scenery and cultural richness.

[Poem Explanation]

The poem beautifully captures the arrival of spring rain and its effects on the natural world. The rain, well-timed with the awakening of plant life in spring, falls quietly during the night, nurturing everything it touches.

The rural paths are shrouded in darkness, concealed by heavy clouds, with only the lights on the riverboats visible.

In the morning, the poet observes the flowers in the city, all laden with the weight of raindrops.

The poet joyfully describes the timely arrival of spring rain and the scenes of Chengdu's nighttime rainfall.

[Reading]

Sound and Verse Regulations for Elementary Studies
The Conical Old Man's Manual of Couplets and Rhythm (Excerpt)

Clouds pair with rain, snow pairs with wind;
Evening glow pairs with clear sky.
Incoming wild swans pair with departing swallows;
Birds at rest pair with singing insects.
A three-foot sword, (pairs) a six-jun bow;
Northern hills pair with eastern rivers.
A serene palace to cool the heat on the earth;
(Pairs) a vast cold palace in the sky.
On both riverbanks, in morning mists poplars and willows are green;
In one garden, after the spring rain the apricot blossoms are red.

[Introduction to *The Conical Old Man's Manual of Couplets and Rhythm*]
The Conical Old Man's Manual of Couplets and Rhythm is authored by the late Ming and early Qing literary figure Li Yu. It is a primer for understanding the principles of poetic rhythm.

第五课

唐诗（二）

将(qiāng)进酒

[唐] 李白

君不见，黄河之水天上来，

奔流到海不复回。

君不见，高堂明镜悲白发，

朝如青丝暮成雪。

人生得意须尽欢，

莫使金樽空对月。

天生我材必有用，

千金散尽还复来。

烹羊宰牛且为乐，

会须一饮三百杯。

岑(cén)夫子，丹丘生，

将进酒，杯莫停。

与君歌一曲,

请君为我倾耳听。

钟鼓馔(zhuàn)玉不足贵,

但愿长醉不愿醒。

古来圣贤皆寂寞,

惟有饮者留其名。

陈王昔时宴平乐(lè),

斗酒十千恣欢谑(xuè)。

王金泰 画

主人何为言少钱,

径须沽取对君酌。

五花马,千金裘,

呼儿将出换美酒,

与尔同销万古愁。

【注释】

  将进酒:将,读作qiāng,请;将进酒,请喝酒。

  岑夫子、丹丘生:李白的两个朋友。

  倾耳听:倾,歪,斜。这里指仔细听。

  钟鼓:乐器名,这里指敲钟鼓作乐。

  馔玉:馔,饮食;玉,指像玉一样美好;馔玉,珍美如玉的饮食。

  圣贤:品格高尚、才智过人的人。

  陈王:曹植。

  平乐:道观名。

  谑:开玩笑。

【讲解】

　　这首诗是在李白初入京城,失意而归,与朋友相会时写下的一首"劝酒歌"。

　　难道你没有看见黄河之水从高天奔流而下,东入大海,如时光奔流不回?难道你没有看见镜中的黑发,转眼间已变为雪白,是多么令人伤悲!然而,人生并不是一杯苦酒,还是和朋友们痛快地饮酒谈笑吧,不要让精美的酒杯空对明月。"天生我材必有用",千金散尽还会有的。功名富贵,不过是过眼云烟。朝廷让人失望,金钱、物品都不必珍惜,只有美酒可以消愁。

　　这首诗虽然流露出诗人对自己得不到重用的感叹,但还是表达了豪放、乐观的情怀,是一首不可多得的好作品,是李白的代表作之一。

生 词

mò 莫	not, don't		xī shí 昔时	in the past
zūn 樽	bottle, goblet		zì 恣	do as one pleases
pēng 烹	cook		gū 沽	buy
qīng tīng 倾听	listen attentively		zhuó 酌	drink
shèng xián 圣贤	sages and men of virtue		qiú 裘	fur coat
jì mò 寂寞	lonesome, lonely		ěr 尔	you
wéi 惟	only		chóu 愁	worry, distress

背诵并默写

《将进酒》的前八句

比一比

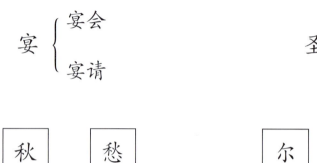

秋	愁		尔	你
秋天	发愁			

反义词

醉——醒　　昔时——将来/来日

寂寞——热闹

词语运用

皆

① 姐姐考上了理想的大学，全家皆大欢喜。

② 春节时，路上皆是快乐的人群。

Lesson Five

Poetry in Tang Dynasty (II)

Invitation to Wine

By Li Bai, Tang Dynasty

Do you not see the Yellow River come from the sky,
Rushing into the sea and never coming back?
Do you not see the mirrors bright in chambers high,
Grieve over the snow-white hair at dusk when at dawn it was silk-black?
We should drink the joy of life to the last drop,
Don't face the moon with an empty golden goblet.
Natural talents like us are surely useful.
A thousand gold pieces are spent,
More will cerlainly come.
Cook the lamb, slaughter the oxen, let us be merry;
Now is the time to drink three hundred cups.

Cen Fuzi, Dan Qiu Sheng, please continue drinking.
Raise your cups without stopping.
A song for you I will sing,
Please listen with ears willing.
What difference will rare and costly dishes make?
I only want to get drunk and never awake.
Since ancient times wise men and sages are all lonely,
Only drinkers leave their names in history.
Once the Prince of Chen feasted in his palace of Peace and Joy,
People drank wine of ten thousand casks and laughed and joked.
No need for the host to complain of lacking money,
I can sell things to buy wine to drink with you.
My fur coat worth a thousand coins of gold,
With my flower-dappled horse can all be sold,
By my servant lad to buy good wine,
We will drink it to drown the sorrow of ages old.

[Annotation]

将进酒："将" pronounced as qiāng, meaning to invite or please; "将进酒" is an invitation to drink.

岑夫子、丹丘生：Li Bai's two friends mentioned in the poem

倾耳听："倾" means to tilt or incline; here it means to listen attentively.

钟鼓：playing musical instruments, creating a joyful atmosphere

馔玉："馔" refers to food and drink; "玉" symbolizes something beautiful; "馔玉" describes exquisite food and drink.

圣贤：virtuous and wise individuals

陈王：Cao Zhi, a historical figure and poet mentioned in the poem

平乐：the name of a Taoist temple

谑：joking or making fun

[Explanation of the Poem]

This poem was composed by Li Bai when he gathered with friends after he first went to the capital but returned disheartened.

Have you not seen the waters of the Yellow River rushing down from the heavens, flowing eastward into the sea, just like the swift passage of time that never turns back? Have you not observed in the mirror how the black hair turns snow-white in the blink of an eye, causing deep sorrow? However, life is not just a bitter cup of wine. Instead, let's joyfully drink and chat with friends, not allowing the exquisite wine cups to be empty beneath the bright moon. "Heaven has bestowed upon me talents that must be utilized;" even if wealth is squandered, there will still be more. Fame and fortune are but fleeting illusions. The disappointment from the court, the disregard for wealth and possessions—these need not be cherished. Only fine wine can dispel sorrows.

This poem is one of Li Bai's masterpieces. While revealing the poet's lament for not receiving due recognition, it conveys a spirit of boldness and optimism, standing as a rare and excellent work.

第六课

宋词（一）

"词"早在唐代就已经有了，但是到了宋代，词才真正流行起来。词按不同的格式填写，句子有长有短，更有表现力。词的创作在宋代达到了高峰。《全宋词》一书收集了两万多首词，其中著名的词作者有苏轼、陆游等。

念奴娇·赤壁怀古[①]

［北宋］苏轼

大江东去，

浪淘尽，

千古风流人物。

故垒西边，

人道是，

三国周郎赤壁。

[①] 念奴娇·赤壁怀古——"念奴娇"是一个词牌名（词调的名称），"赤壁怀古"是词的题目。赤壁，地名，在今中国湖北省。

乱石穿空，

惊涛拍岸，

卷起千堆雪。

江山如画，

一时多少豪杰。

遥想公瑾(jǐn)当年，

小乔初嫁了(liǎo)，

雄姿英发。

羽扇纶(guān)巾，

谈笑间，

樯橹(qiáng lǔ)灰飞烟灭。

故国神游，

多情应笑我，

早生华发。

人生如梦，

一尊还酹(lèi)江月。

王金泰　画

【注释】

怀古：追念古代的事情。

风流人物：这里指英雄人物。

故垒：古代军营的墙壁或工事。

周郎：指周瑜(yú)。

公瑾：周瑜的字。

小乔：周瑜的妻子，三国时期最有名的美人之一。

雄姿：英武的样子。

纶巾：古代配有青丝带的头巾。

樯橹：代指曹操的水军。樯，挂帆的桅杆。橹，安装在船尾可使船前进的工具。

酹：把酒洒在地上，表示纪念。

【讲解】

这是苏轼游赤壁时写下的一首名作。

历史如滚滚东流的长江水，后浪推前浪，永不停息。千百年来，这里发生过惊天动地的战事，涌(yǒng)现出非凡的英雄！江岸上古代营垒的西边，听说是三国周瑜大破曹军的赤壁古战场。那里巨石直入云间，大浪拍着岸边，层层浪花像一堆堆白雪。真是江山如画，豪杰辈出！

回想周瑜当年，美丽的小乔刚嫁给他。周瑜年轻英武，与诸葛亮在谈笑中定出了攻打曹军的计划，一把火烧得曹军战船灰飞烟灭。诗人游古战场，笑自己太动情了，早早白了头发。他感叹：人生短暂(zàn)如梦！便把酒倒入江中，祭(jì)月亮吧！

作者简介

苏轼（1037—1101），北宋时期文学家、书法家、画家，在中国文学史上占有重要地位。在诗词创作方面，他开创了豪放词派，对后世有很大的影响。《念奴娇·赤壁怀古》是千古传诵的杰作，也是苏轼的代表作之一。后人用这个词调的时候，有的就用"大江东去"或"酹江月"来代替"念奴娇"，由此可见这首词的名气和影响有多大！

生词

gé shi 格式	format	duī 堆	pile
sū shì 苏轼	Su Shi, a person's name	háo jié 豪杰	hero
nú 奴	slave	qiáo 乔	Joe
táo 淘	wash	zī 姿	posture
tāo 涛	big waves		

背诵并默写

《念奴娇·赤壁怀古》前十一行

比一比

嫁（出嫁）　　　格式　　　雄姿
家（家庭）　格　格子　　姿　姿势

多音字

juǎn
卷

风卷着乌云。
岸边停放的小船，被海浪卷走了。

juàn
卷

《本草纲目》全书共52卷。
老师拿着考卷走进教室。

词语解释

江山——江河和山岭，常用来指国家。

Lesson Six

Song Ci (I)

"Ci" already existed as early as the Tang Dynasty, but it was in the Song Dynasty that it truly gained popularity. Written in various formats with sentences of different lengths, Ci became even more expressive than Shi. The creation of Ci reached its peak in the Song Dynasty. The book *Complete Collection of Song Ci* gathers over 20,000 pieces of Ci, with the most renowned Ci authors being Su Shi, Lu You, and many others.

Nian Nu Jiao: Recall the Past at Red Cliff
By Su Shi, the Northern Song Dynasty

East flows the mighty river,
Its waves sweeping away the great heroes of all times.
To the west of this ancient rampart,
People say is the Red Cliff of Zhou Yu during Three Kingdoms.

Jagged rocks pierce the sky,
Startling waves beat the shore,
Rolling up a thousand piles of snowing foams.
The river and mountains look like a picture,
In history how many heroes have emerged!

Think of Gongjin back in those days
who just married Xiaoqiao the beauty charming,
A hero so handsome and dashing!
A feather fan in his hand and silk headbanded,
In casual conversing and jesting,
Strong enemy forces were beaten in ashes flying and smoke dissipating.

Daydreaming of the old times,
I shall be mocked at these feelings overflowing,
No wonder my hair is prematurely graying.

Life is like a dream,
I fill a cup and toast to the river and the moon.

[Annotation]

怀古：to memorialize the ancient things
风流人物：here refers to heroes and heroines
故垒：the wall or fortification of an ancient military camp
周郎：referring to Zhou Yu
公瑾：Zhou Yu's courtesy name
小乔：wife of Zhou Yu, one of the most famous beauties of the Three Kingdoms period
雄姿：a heroic appearance
纶巾：an ancient turban with a green ribbon
樯橹：樯：a sailing mast; 橹：an installation at the stern of a boat that propels the boat forward
酹：spilling wine on the ground to commemorate the occasion

[Explanation of the Poem]

This is a masterpiece written by Su Shi when he visited the Red Cliff.

History is like the Yangtze River rolling eastward, the latter waves pushing the former waves, never stopping, never ending. For thousands of years, this has seen innumerable earth-shattering battles and extraordinary heroes! The west side of the ancient fortress on the river bank is said to be the ancient battlefield of Red Cliff where Zhou Yu of the Three Kingdoms defeated Cao's army. There, huge boulders rise into the clouds, big waves lap at the shore, and layers of waves look like piles of white snow. The river and mountains form a wonderful picture in which many great men and women come and go.

He think of Zhou Yu, who was young and handsome and the beautiful Xiao Qiao just married him. He recalled Zhuge Liang who laughingly conjured the plan to attack Cao's army, a fire burned Cao's warships to ashes. The poet traveled to the ancient battlefield, and then laughed at himself for being too emotional and had early gray hair as a result.

He lamented that life was just like a dream. Then he poured the wine into the river, offering it to the moon.

[About the Author]

Su Shi (1037-1101), a great writer, calligrapher, and painter of the Northern Song Dynasty, occupies an important position in the history of Chinese literature. In terms of poetic creation, he pioneered the school of bold and unrestrained lyricism, which had a great influence on later generations. *Nian Nu jiao: Recall the Past at Red Cliff*（念奴娇·赤壁怀古）, one of Su Shi's masterpieces, has been recited throughout the ages. When the later generations use this tune, some of them use the words "Going East of the Great River" or "Sprinkling the Moon" instead of "Nian Nu jiao," which shows how famous and influential this piece of poetic lyric is.

第七课

宋词（二）

钗头凤①

[南宋] 陆游

红酥手，黄縢(téng)酒，

满城春色宫墙柳。

东风恶，欢情薄，

一怀愁绪，几年离索。

错！错！错！

春如旧，人空瘦，

泪痕红浥(yì)鲛(jiāo)绡(xiāo)透。

桃花落，闲池阁，

山盟虽在，锦书难托。

莫！莫！莫！

---

① 钗头凤——词牌名。

第七课

王金泰　画

【注释】

红酥手：指女人细软的手。

黄縢酒：古代的一种酒。

东风：这里比喻诗人的母亲。

欢情薄：指美满的爱情遭到破坏。

一怀愁绪：满心的愁苦。

离索：别离。

春如旧，人空瘦：春天如期而至，只是人憔悴(qiáo cuì)消瘦。

泪痕红浥鲛绡透：浥，沾湿；鲛绡，手帕(pà)。泪水湿透了手帕。

山盟虽在，锦书难托：爱情誓言还在，可无法写信表达。

【讲解】

陆游早年娶唐琬(wǎn)为妻,两人十分恩爱。但陆游的母亲不喜欢唐琬,把他们分开了。几年后的一个春日,陆游在家乡的沈园遇到已嫁人的唐琬,心中悲伤,在沈园的墙壁上写下了这首《钗头凤》。

柔软的手拿着盛有黄縢酒的杯子,满城春花,宫墙绿柳。东风寒冷,吹走了幸福。满心的愁苦,几年的离别。感叹:错,错,错!

春天如期而至,可心上人已憔悴消瘦。泪水滴落,手帕湿透。桃花散落,池边楼阁冷冷清清。相爱的誓言还在心中,可信已不能写了。感叹:莫,莫,莫!

作者简介

陆游(1125—1210),南宋爱国诗人。他生活的时代,正是南宋不断受到金国入侵(qīn)的时代。陆游也做过官,坚决主张抗金。他一生留下九千多首诗,其中许多诗反映了他抗金爱国的热情。

生词

chāi		lèi hén	
钗	hairpin, *an ornament formerly worn by women*	泪痕	tear trace

shān méng　hǎi shì
山盟（海誓）a solemn pledge of love

qíng　xù
（情）绪　mood

背诵并默写

《钗头凤》全词

比一比

痕 { 泪痕
　　　痕迹

闲 { 清闲
　　　休闲

词语运用

情绪

① 比赛之前，队员们情绪高涨，信心十足。

② 弟弟考试没考好就闹情绪。

托

① 老师让我先去看病，作业托同学带给我。

② 我们出去旅游，托姑姑帮忙照看房子。

词语解释

山盟海誓——男女相爱立下的誓言和盟约，表示爱情要像山和海那样永远不变。

阅读

钗头凤

[南宋] 唐琬

世情薄，人情恶，
雨送黄昏花易落。
晓风干，泪痕残，
欲笺心事，独语斜阑。
难！难！难！

王金泰　画

人成各，今非昨，

病魂常似秋千索。

角声寒，夜阑珊，

怕人寻问，咽泪装欢。

瞒！瞒！瞒！

【注释】

晓风：晨风。

泪痕残：脸上留下眼泪的痕迹。

欲笺心事：想要写信说说心事。

斜阑：这里"阑"同"栏"。斜阑，斜靠着栏杆。

人成各，今非昨：现在不比以前，她与陆游已成为互不相干的两个人了。

秋千索：秋千的绳子。

角声寒：号角声凄凉。

夜阑珊：阑珊，将尽；夜阑珊，黑夜快要过去了。

【讲解】

对唐琬来说，世间的人情太冷、太薄。她与陆游这对恩爱夫妻被婆婆活活拆散。她觉得自己就像在黄昏中被风雨吹打的花，满身是伤。一夜夜的泪水，一次次地被晨风吹干，满心的痛苦又能向谁诉说？只能独自靠

着栏杆叹息："难！难！难！"

唐琬感到自己的命运就像秋千上的绳子，飘飘荡荡，不能自主。更不幸的是唐琬改嫁后，连表达悲苦的自由都没有了。长夜无眠，听着凄凉的号角声，让人心碎，直到天明，又"怕人寻问，咽泪装欢"，只能"瞒！瞒！瞒！"

据说唐琬作此词后不久就去世了。这首词表达了她对封建礼法的不满和内心的巨大痛苦。如泣如诉，真切感人。

Lesson Seven

Song Ci (II)

Phoenix Hairpin

By Lu You, Southern Song Dynasty

Soft red-fingernailed hands,
Hold a cup of yellow corded wine.
Under the garden walls the willow trees stand,
The entire city enjoys spring time.
The east wind is so harsh blowing away our joy so thin.
My heart is full of sorrowful thoughts over years of separation and longing.
Wrong! Wrong! Wrong!

It's a similar spring,
Yet my beloved is thinning.
Her tears leave traces on the red silk handkerchief.
Peach blossoms fall; pavilions by the pond we could visit no more.
Though our love oath still stands,
Sending you a letter is difficult.
No! No! No!

[Annotation]

红酥手：red, tender hands, refers to the delicate hands of a woman

黄縢酒：yellow, silk-bound wine, an ancient type of wine

东风：east wind, metaphorically refers to the poet's mother

欢情薄：joy is thin, suggests that the joy in life is fleeting and short-lived

一怀愁绪：a heart full of sorrows and thoughts, describes a heart filled with melancholy and sad thoughts

离索：separation and longing

春如旧，人空瘦：spring is as before; yet the person is thinning.

泪痕红浥鲛绡透：tears leave red traces on the soaked delicate silk, depicts tears staining a handkerchief. 浥：stained by tears；鲛绡：handker chief

山盟虽在，锦书难托：though the love oath still stands, sending a brocade letter is difficult.

despite promises, expressing love becomes challenging.

[Explanation of the Poem]

In his early years, Lu You married Tang Wan. They shared a deeply and loving relationship. However, Lu You's mother disapproved of Tang Wan and forced Lu You to divorce her. Several years later, on a spring day in his hometown Hangzhou at Shen Garden, Lu You encountered Tang Wan, now married to someone else. Overwhelmed with sorrow, he wrote the poem "钗头凤" (*Phoenix Hairpin*) on the wall of Shen Garden.

The poet describes the scene of Tang Wan's delicate hands holding cups of yellow colored wine, offering him to drink beside the garden walls adorned with spring flowers and green willows. The cold east wind (his mother) blows away Tang Wan and their happiness. The poet can only lament the deep sorrows in his heart accumulated over the years of separation. He expresses his anguish with the repeated exclamation "错，错，错！" (Wrong, wrong, wrong!).

Despite the arrival of spring, his beloved ex-wife has become gaunt. Tears fall from his eyes, soaking the red silk handkerchief. Peach blossoms scatter and the pavilions by the pond appear desolate. The vows of love are still in his heart, but it is impossible to send her a letter telling her his love. The poet sighs with the repeated exclamation "莫，莫，莫！" (No, no, no!), emphasizing the difficulty of conveying his feelings.

[Author's Biography]

陆游 (Lu You) (1125-1210):

Lu You was a patriotic poet of the Southern Song Dynasty in China. He lived during a tumultuous period when the Southern Song Dynasty faced continuous invasions from the Jin Dynasty. Lu You also served as an official and was a staunch advocate for resisting the Jin Dynasty's aggression. Throughout his life, he composed over nine thousand poems, many of which reflected his fervent patriotism and his commitment to resisting the invading forces of the Jin Dynasty.

[Reading]

Phoenix Hairpin

By Tang Wan, Southern Song

In this world, emotions are shallow, and people's hearts are wicked.
Rain falls at dusk; flowers easily wither.
Morning wind dries, leaving traces of tears behind.
Wanting to write down what is on my mind,
I stand alone and speak to myself by the tilted window.
Difficult! Difficult! Difficult!

We have become separate,
Today is different from yesterday.

My ailing soul is like a swing rope.
The sound of the horn brings coldness,
The night is almost over.
Afraid of others looking for me and asking,
 I swallow my tears and fake happiness.
Conceal! Conceal! Conceal!

[Annotation]
晓风：morning wind, refers to the breeze in the morning
泪痕残：traces of tears remaining, describes the marks or traces of tears left on the face
欲笺心事：wanting to record what's in the mind, expresses the desire to write down one's innermost thoughts or feelings in a letter
斜阑：tilted window, here "阑" is synonymous with "栏" (railing or fence). "斜阑" suggests leaning or tilting against the railing.
人成各，今非昨：we are separate and not a couple anymore, today is different from yesterday, implies that people change, and the present is different from the past, indicating the separation between the writer and Lu You
秋千索：swing's swinging ropes, refers to the ropes of a swing, symbolizing the ups and downs or uncertainties of feelings and life
角声寒：the sound of footsteps is cold, conveys a sense of desolation and coldness in the sound of approaching footsteps
夜阑珊：night is ending, "阑珊" suggests that the night is coming to an end, and dawn is approaching

[Explanation of the Poem]
For Tang Wan, the sentiments of the world are too cold and thin. Lu You and she, although deeply in love with each other, were forced to separate by the mother-in-law. She felt like a flower battered by wind and rain in the twilight, covered in wounds. Night after night, the morning wind blew her tears dry. She had no one to confide her pain in. Alone, she leaned against the railing, sighing, "Difficult! Difficult! Difficult!"

Tang Wan perceived her destiny like the swinging ropes of a swing, drifting aimlessly, lacking autonomy. Sadly after her second marriage, she lost even the freedom to express her sorrow. Sleepless nights, listening to the desolate sound of horns, enduring the pain of a broken heart until dawn. Yet, she "fears inquiries from others, swallows tears pretending to be joyful," and can only "Conceal! Conceal! Conceal!"

It is said that Tang Wan passed away not long after composing this poem. The poem expresses her discontent with feudal customs and her immense inner pain. Like weeping and narrating, the poem is deeply touching.

第八课

宋词（三）

满江红①·写怀

〔南宋〕 岳飞

怒发冲冠，

凭栏处、

潇潇雨歇。

抬望眼、

仰天长啸，

壮怀激烈。

三十功名尘与土，

八千里路云和月。

莫等闲、

白了少年头，

空悲切。

---

① 满江红——词牌名。

靖(jīng)康耻，

犹未雪。

臣子恨，

何时灭。

驾长车踏破、

贺兰山缺。

壮志饥餐胡虏肉，

笑谈渴饮匈奴血。

待从头、

收拾旧山河，

朝天阙(què)。

王金泰 画

【注释】

凭栏：靠着栏杆。

潇潇：雨声。

啸：这里指长声喊叫。

壮怀激烈：壮志在心中激荡。

等闲：随随便便；轻易。

白了少年头：青少年变成了白发老人。

空悲切：一事无成而伤心悲哀。

靖康耻：指靖康元年（1126）金军攻下宋朝首都，第二年又掳走宋朝皇帝等三千多人，北宋灭亡。

犹未雪：（耻辱 rǔ）还没洗掉。

贺兰山缺：贺兰山，山名，在中国西北。缺，缺口，这里指山口。

胡虏：外敌，这里指金国人。

匈奴：这里指中国北方、西北地区的民族，主要指金国人。

朝天阙：阙 liào，宫门两边的瞭望楼，代表皇宫；朝天阙，朝见皇帝。

【讲解】

潇潇的细雨停了，岳飞站在高处的栏杆前，放眼远望，悲愤之情从心中涌出；抬起头向着长空大喊一声，要打败金兵收复国土的壮志在心中激荡。他回想一生转战万里抗敌报国的经历，更感到收复失地的紧迫，不能白白地浪费时间了。

他想到靖康年的国耻至今未报，作为国家的大臣，内心怎能平静呢？他要驾着战车直冲到贺兰山下，与敌人决一死战。等到打败了敌人的那一天，再重新修建可爱的家园。

这是一首千古杰作，表达了岳飞希望报仇雪恨、收复国土的悲壮心情。

作者简介

岳飞（1103—1142），南宋抗金名将。他主张抗金，带领南宋军队多次打败金军，收复失去的疆土。但是皇帝和大臣秦桧(huì)一心求和，将岳飞杀害。

生 词

nù 怒	anger, fury		jià 驾	drive
xiāo xiāo 潇潇	drizzlingly		tà 踏	step on, tread
xiào 啸	roar, howl		jī 饥	hungry
jī liè 激烈	fervent, violent		hú lǔ 胡虏	enemy
chén 尘	dust		xiōng nú 匈奴	Hsiung-Nu (*an ancient nationality in China*)
chǐ 耻	shame		shōu shi 收拾	pack, recover
yóu 犹	still			

背诵并默写

《满江红·写怀》前十一行

比一比

耻 { 可耻 / 耻辱 }   激 { 激烈 / 激动 }

反义词

激烈——温和   耻辱——光荣

词语运用

闲

① 等考完试闲下来，我们就去旅游。

② 妈妈下班回家马上忙着做饭，一分钟都闲不下来。

驾

① 下雨天驾车，要特别注意安全。

② 开车要有驾照。

词语解释

怒发冲冠——头发直竖，把帽子都顶起来了。形容非常愤怒。

夏日绝句

〔南宋〕李清照

生当为人杰，
死亦为鬼雄。
至今思项羽，
不肯过江东。

【注释】

人杰：人中豪杰。

鬼雄：鬼中英雄。

项羽：西楚霸王，与刘邦争夺天下，后兵败自杀。

江东：长江以南的地区，项羽起兵的地方。

【讲解】

生时应当做人中豪杰，死后也要做鬼中英雄。
到今天人们还在怀念项羽，因为他不肯渡(dù)江回到江东。

作者简介

李清照（1084—约1155），宋朝人，中国历史上著名的女词人。

Lesson Eight

Song Ci (III)

Full River Red: Writing from the Heart
By Yue Fei, Southern Song Dynasty

Fury erects my hair which heightens my hat,
I lean on the railing, watching the drizzlingly rain slowly stop.
Lifting my gaze,
I heave a long roar towards the sky,
Out of my fervent and passionate mind.
Thirty years of fame is nothing more than the dust on the ground,
I traveled eight thousand li under the clouds and moonlight.
Don't idle,
When the young head turned gray,
One will regret it to no avail.
The great shame of the year of JingKang,
Is not yet revenged.
The hate of all officials,
When can it be quenched?
Driving the battle chariots,
Break through the Hill of Helan.
Valiantly we will eat our foe's meat when hungry,
Laughing and talking we will drink the blood of our enemy when thirsty.
Let us start anew!
Let us recover our lost land,
In triumph we will return our army to the palace grand.

[Annotation]
凭栏：leaning on the railing, standing by the railing
潇潇：the sound of a gentle rain, 其他：describes the sound of rain
啸：roar, in this context it refers to a long and loud shout
壮怀激烈：fervent and passionate spirit, describes a strong and intense aspiration or determination

等闲：don't idle away, indicating not to pass time casually or carelessly

白了少年头：the young head turning prematurely gray, symbolizing the premature aging of a young person, possibly due to hardships or struggles

空悲切：empty and full of sorrow, expressing a sense of deep sadness and regret over unfulfilled aspirations

靖康耻：shame of Jingkang, referring to the events of the first year of the Jingkang era (1126), during which the Jin Dynasty captured the capital of the Song Dynasty. The following year, the Jin Dynasty abducted over three thousand individuals, including the emperor, leading to the downfall of the Northern Song Dynasty.

犹未雪：still not avenged, indicates that the shame or disgrace has not been wiped away

贺兰山缺：gap in the Helan Mountains. Helan Mountains, a mountain range in northwestern China. "缺" here refers to a gap or pass in the mountains.

胡虏：invaders/enemies from the north, refers to foreign enemies, specifically the Jin Dynasty

匈奴：Hsiung-Nu, in this context, it symbolizes various northern and northwestern ethnic groups, often used to refer to the Jin Dynasty.

朝天阙："阙" refers to a watchtower on each side of the palace gate. "朝天阙" means paying respect to the emperor.

[Explanation of the Poem]

The gentle rain has stopped, Yue Fei stands by the railing at a high place, gazes into the distance, and a surge of sorrow and resentment wells up in his heart. Lifting his head towards the vast sky, he shouts, expressing his resolute ambition to defeat the Jin forces and reclaim the lost territories. Reflecting on a lifetime of campaigning across vast distances to resist enemies and serve the country, Yue Fei feels the urgency to recover the lost lands. He senses that time can't be wasted, especially considering the unavenged national shame endured during the Jingkang era. As a loyal minister of the nation, he can't find peace at heart. Yue Fei envisions driving his war chariot straight to the foot of the Helan Mountains, ready to engage in a decisive battle against the enemy. He is determined to fight until the day of victory, at which point he plans to rebuild the beloved homeland that has been lost.

This is an enduring masterpiece that conveys Yue Fei's poignant emotions of seeking revenge, avenging grievances, and reclaiming lost territories.

[Author's Biography]

Yue Fei (1103-1142) was a renowned military general during the Southern Song Dynasty, known for his resistance against the Jin Dynasty. He advocated for opposing the Jin forces and led the Southern Song army to numerous victories and reclaimed lost territories. However, the emperor and his minister Qin Hui, who were bent on seeking negotiation with Jin, killed Yue Fei.

[Selective]

Summary Day, a Quatrain

By Li Qingzhao, Southern Song Dynasty

When alive, a man should be a hero.
When dead, be a ghost of valor.
Until now I still think of Xiang Yu,
Who would rather die than cross the river eastward.

[Annotation]
人杰：hero among men
鬼雄：hero among ghosts
项羽：Xiang Yu, the overlord of Western Chu, who contended with Liu Bang for dominion, later met defeat and took his own life.
江东：the region to the south of the Yangtze River, where Xiang Yu initiated his uprising

[Explanation of the Poem]
In life, one should strive to be a hero among men. After death, one should become a valiant ghost among spirits. Up to now people still remember Xiang Yu, the overlord of Western Chu, because he chose to kill himself in defeat instead of crossing the river to go back to his hometown in the east.

[Author's Biography]
Li Qingzhao (1084-about 1155) was a renowned female poet during the Song Dynasty, widely celebrated in Chinese history for her exceptional poetry of Ci.

第九课

古诗词二首

相见欢①

[南唐] 李煜(yù)

王金泰　画

无言独上西楼，
月如钩。
寂寞梧桐深院锁清秋。

剪不断，
理还乱，
是离愁。
别是一番滋味在心头。

---

① 相见欢——词牌名。

【注释】

离愁：离别之苦。

【讲解】

独自登上西楼，静静地遥望茫茫夜空，一弯残月，照着庭院里的梧桐。这样寂寞、冷清的秋色也被锁在高墙深院中。然而，锁住的又何止是这满院的秋色？诗人心乱如麻："剪不断，理还乱，是离愁。"这种愁苦的滋味真是说不出的难受啊！

作者简介

李煜（937—978），南唐最后一位皇帝，也是一位杰出的词人。他当皇帝时，南唐国力已经很弱，而宋强大起来。他一方面为讨好宋朝，每年送金银等物，另一方面又在生活上尽情享乐。后来，南唐被宋所灭，他自己也成了囚(qiú)徒。这首《相见欢》就是他被囚禁之时写的。

题都城南庄

［唐］崔护

去年今日此门中，

人面桃花相映红。

人面不知何处去，

桃花依旧笑春风。

【讲解】

　　崔护去城南游玩，见到一户农家院中有一棵桃树，桃花盛开伸出墙外。不想开门的是一位美丽的姑娘，面如桃花，使人难忘。第二年，他又来到这户农家，但美丽的姑娘已经不见了，只有院中的桃花依旧在春风中摇摆(bǎi)。

生词

gōu 钩	hook		tí 题	inscribe
wú tóng 梧桐	Chinese parasol tree		zhuāng 庄	village
suǒ 锁	lock up		cuī 崔	Cui, a surname
fān 番	a kind of ; times		yìng 映	reflect
zī wèi 滋味	taste, flavor			

背诵并默写

《相见欢》《题都城南庄》

比一比

钩 { 钩子 / 鱼钩 }   题 { 考题 / 做题 }

词语运用

锁

① 晚上睡觉前,要把门锁好。

② 崔护发现大门是锁着的。

③ 这种旅行箱上的锁是号码锁。

滋味

① 今天考试没考好,心里真不是滋味。

② 我病了,身上不舒服,吃饭一点儿滋味都没有。

咏 柳

［唐］贺知章

碧玉妆成一树高,
万条垂下绿丝绦(tāo)。
不知细叶谁裁(cái)出,
二月春风似剪刀。

【注释】

碧玉：碧绿色的玉。这里比喻春天嫩绿的柳叶。

妆：打扮。

一树：满树。

绦：用丝编成的绳带。这里指像丝带一样的柳条。

裁：裁剪。

【讲解】

春天嫩绿的叶子把柳树打扮起来，柳枝垂下像万条绿色丝带。
这细细的柳叶是谁剪的呀？二月春风就像一把灵巧的剪刀。

这是一首七言绝句，描写了诗人对春天到来的喜悦，又用拟人写法将"二月春风"比喻为"剪刀"十分巧妙。

Lesson Nine

Two Classical Poems

To the Tune of *Xiangjianhuan* (*Happy Reunion*)
By Li Yu, Southern Tang Dynasty

Silently and alone, I ascend the western tower,
Like a hook hangs the moon.
The lonely parasol tree stands in the deep courtyard locked in the clear autumn.

My sorrow of parting,
Is unable to cut off.
It only gets more entangled after sorting.
My heart must endure this terrible feeling.

[Annotation]
离愁：The sorrow of parting or separation.

[Explanation of the Poem]
Alone, I ascend the western tower, silently gazing into the vast night sky. A waning crescent moon shines upon the parasol trees in the courtyard. This lonely and desolate autumn scene seems to be locked within the high walls and deep courtyards.

However, what is truly "locked" extends beyond just the autumn scenery filling the courtyard. The poet's heart is in turmoil, tangled and disturbed: "Unable to cut off, thoughts remain entangled, it's the sorrow of parting." The taste of this sorrow is indescribably difficult to endure.

[Author's Biography]
Li Yu (937–978) was the last emperor of the Southern Tang Dynasty and a distinguished Ci poet. During his reign, the Southern Tang Dynasty was very weak, while the Song Dynasty was rising in power. Li Yu attempted to appease the Song Dynasty by sending annual tributes, including gold and silver, while indulging in a life of pleasure. Later, the Southern Tang Dynasty was conquered by the Song Dynasty, and Li Yu himself became a prisoner. This poem, *Happy Reunion* was written during his captivity.

Inscription at the Southern Villa of the Capital

By Cui Hu, Tang Dynasty

On this day last year, within this gate,
The pink peach blossoms shined with her beauliful face.
I know not now where she is,
Only the peach blossoms still smile in spring breeze.

[Explanation of the Poem]

On the Qingming Festival, Cui Hu went to the southern part of the capital where he approached a farmhouse. In the courtyard of this farmhouse, there was a flourishing peach tree with its blossoms extending beyond the wall. The door opened, revealing a beautiful maiden with a face like peach blossoms, leaving a lasting impression on Cui Hu.

The following year, on the same Qingming Festival, he visited the farmhouse again, the peach blossoms in the farmhouse courtyard still swayed in the spring breeze, yet the deeply cherished maiden from the poet's heart was nowhere to be seen.

[Selective]

Ode to the Willow Tree

By He Zhizhang, Tang Dynasty

Green jade adorns this tree tall and lofty,
Countless branches hang down like ribbons green and silky.
I wonder who fashioned these delicate leaves.
February's spring breeze acts as the scissors.

[Annotation]
碧玉：jade-green, metaphorically used to describe the tender green willow leaves in spring
妆：adorn or dress up
一树：an entire tree
绦：silk threads or ribbons, here referring to willow branches resembling ribbons
裁：cut or trim

[Explanation of the Poem]
Spring adorns the willow tree with tender green leaves, and its branches hang down like countless green silk ribbons. The poet wonders who crafted these delicate willow leaves. In February, the spring breeze acts as a skillful pair of scissors.

   This is a seven-character quatrain that expresses the poet's joy at the arrival of spring. The use of personification, portraying the "February spring breeze" as a pair of scissors, adds a clever touch to the poem.

第十课

现代诗

现代诗也叫"白话诗",最早可追源到清末,是诗歌的一种,与古典诗歌相比,现代诗形式自由,一般不拘格式和韵律。

乡 愁

余光中

小时候

乡愁是一枚小小的邮票

我在这头

母亲在那头

长大后

乡愁是一张窄窄的船票

我在这头

新娘在那头

后来呵

乡愁是一方矮矮的坟墓

我在外头

母亲呵在里头

而现在

乡愁是一湾浅浅的海峡

我在这头

大陆在那头

作品简介

  《乡愁》是台湾著名诗人余光中先生于1971年所写。诗歌抒发了他内心难以排解的思念故乡和亲人的感情。诗虽不长，却句句动人。

第十课

生 词

jū 拘	restrain, restrict	wān 湾	bay
yùn lù 韵律	rhythm	hǎi xiá 海峡	strait
méi 枚	piece, measure word		

背诵并默写

《乡愁》

比一比

{ 湾（海湾）
  弯（弯腰） }

{ 句子
  拘束 }

反义词

宽——窄　　　　　深——浅

多音字

曲 (qū) 弯曲

曲 (qǔ) 歌曲

词语解释

乡愁——思乡之愁。

海峡——这里指台湾海峡。

阅读

《黄河颂》（节选）

光未然

我站在高山之巅(diān)，

望黄河滚滚，

奔向东南。

从昆仑山下奔向黄海之边；

把中原大地劈成南北两面。

啊！黄河！

你是中华民族的摇篮！

五千年的古国文化，

从你这儿发源；

多少英雄的故事，

在你身边扮演！

王金泰　画

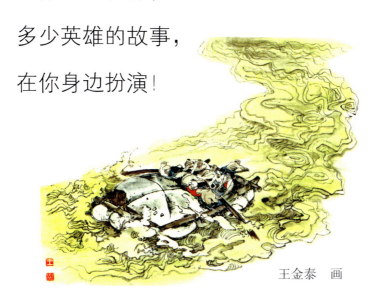

王金泰　画

【注释】

中原：指黄河中下游地区。

作品简介

　　《黄河大合唱》创作于抗日战争时期（1939年3月），由年轻的诗人光未然作词，冼（xiǎn）星海作曲。《黄河颂》是《黄河大合唱》中的一个乐章，也是中华民族的颂歌。它以中华民族的发源地之一——黄河为背景，歌颂了中华民族的古老、伟大和坚强，中华儿女对这片土地的深爱之情以及中华儿女永不屈服的精神。《黄河大合唱》气吞山河，具有鲜明的民族风格，是中国著名的交响音乐。

Lesson Ten

Modern Poetry

Modern poetry, also known as "vernacular poetry," can be traced back to the late Qing Dynasty. It is a form of poetry that, in comparison to classical poetry, features a more liberated form and generally does not adhere to specific formats or rhyme schemes.

Nostalgia for Home

Yu Guangzhong

In childhood,
Nostalgia for home is a tiny postage stamp.
I am on this side;
Mother is on the other side.

Growing up,
Nostalgia for home is a narrow boat ticket.
I am on this side;
My bride is on the other side.

Later, oh,
Nostalgia for home is a small and low tomb.
I am on the outside;
Mother, oh, is inside.

And now,
Nostalgia for home is a shallow strait.
I am on this side;
The mainland is on the other side.

[Introduction to the Work]
Nostalgia for Home (《乡愁》) is a poem written by the renowned Taiwan poet Mr. Yu Guangzhong in 1971. The poem expresses his deep and unresolved feelings of longing for his hometown and loved

ones. Although the poem is not lengthy, every line is poignant with emotion and deeply moving.

[Reading]

Hymn to the Yellow River (excerpt)

Guang Weiran

I stand at the summit of the high mountain,
Gazing at the rolling Yellow River,
Rushing towards the southeast.
From below the Kunlun Mountains,
it flows towards the edge of the Yellow Sea;
Dividing the Central Plains into the north and south.
Ah! Yellow River!
You are the cradle of the Chinese nation!
The ancient culture of a five-thousand-year-old country originates from you;
Countless heroic stories unfold by your side.

[Annotation]
中原：Central Plains, refers to the area downstream of the Yellow River

[Introduction to the work]
Yellow River Cantata was created during the War against Japanese Aggression (March 1939). It was written by the young poet Guang Weiran and composed by Xian Xinghai. *Hymn to the Yellow River* is a movement within the *Yellow River Cantata* and serves as an anthem for the Chinese nation. Set against the backdrop of one of the origins of the Chinese nation—the Yellow River—it praises the ancient, great, and resilient aspects of the Chinese nation. It also celebrates the deep love and unwavering spirit of the Chinese people for this land. *Yellow River Cantata* is a grand and distinctly nationalistic symphonic music piece renowned in China.

生字表（简）

1. 宴(yàn) 述(shù) 雎(jū) 鸠(jiū) 窈(yǎo) 窕(tiǎo) 淑(shū) 逑(qiú) 彼(bǐ) 兮(xī) 萧(xiāo) 艾(ài)

2. 屈(qū) 漫(màn) 础(chǔ) 逐(zhú) 愤(fèn) 索(suǒ) 联(lián) 抵(dǐ) 歇(xiē) 撒(sǎ) 粽(zòng)

3. 泛(fàn) 亦(yì) 帖(tiě) 替(tì) 征(zhēng) 骏(jùn) 暮(mù) 唤(huàn) 赴(fù) 欲(yù) 阁(gé) 裳(cháng) 伴(bàn) 皆(jiē) 吟(yín) 孟(mèng) 郊(jiāo) 慈(cí)

4. 律(lǜ) 言(yán) 瀑(pù) 乃(nǎi) 潜(qián) 锦(jǐn)

5. 莫(mò) 樽(zūn) 烹(pēng) 倾(qīng) 圣(shèng) 贤(xián) 寂(jì) 寞(mò) 惟(wéi) 昔(xī) 恣(zì) 沽(gū) 酌(zhuó) 裘(qiú) 愁(chóu)

6. 轼(shì) 奴(nú) 淘(táo) 涛(tāo) 堆(duī) 乔(qiáo) 杰(jié) 姿(zī)

7. 钗(chāi) 绪(xù) 盟(méng) 誓(shì)

8. 怒(nù) 潇(xiāo) 啸(xiào) 激(jī) 烈(liè) 尘(chén) 耻(chǐ) 犹(yóu) 驾(jià) 踏(tà) 饥(jī) 虏(lǔ) 匈(xiōng) 拾(shí)

9. 钩(gōu) 梧(wú) 桐(tóng) 锁(suǒ) 番(fān) 滋(zī) 味(wèi) 崔(cuī) 映(yìng)

10. 拘(jū) 枚(méi) 湾(wān) 峡(xiá)

共计101个生字

生字表（繁）

1. 宴(yàn) 述(shù) 雎(jū) 鳩(jiū) 窈(yǎo) 窕(tiǎo) 淑(shū) 逑(qiú) 彼(bǐ) 兮(xī) 蕭(xiāo) 艾(ài)

2. 屈(qū) 漫(màn) 礎(chǔ) 逐(zhú) 憤(fèn) 索(suǒ) 聯(lián) 抵(dǐ) 歇(xiē) 撒(sǎ) 粽(zòng)

3. 泛(fàn) 亦(yì) 帖(tiě) 替(tì) 征(zhēng) 駿(jùn) 暮(mù) 喚(huàn) 赴(fù) 欲(yù) 閣(gé) 裳(cháng) 伴(bàn) 皆(jiē)

    吟(yín) 孟(mèng) 郊(jiāo) 慈(cí)

4. 律(lǜ) 言(yán) 瀑(pù)

    乃(nǎi) 潛(qián) 錦(jǐn)

5. 莫(mò) 樽(zūn) 烹(pēng) 傾(qīng) 聖(shèng) 賢(xián) 寂(jì) 寞(mò) 惟(wéi) 昔(xī) 恣(zì) 沽(gū)

    酌(zhuó) 裘(qiú) 愁(chóu)

6. 軾(shì) 奴(nú) 淘(táo) 濤(tāo) 堆(duī) 喬(qiáo) 傑(jié) 姿(zī)

7. 釵(chāi) 緒(xù) 盟(méng) 誓(shì)

8. 怒(nù) 瀟(xiāo) 嘯(xiào) 激(jī) 烈(liè) 塵(chén) 恥(chǐ) 猶(yóu) 駕(jià) 踏(tà) 饑(jī) 虜(lǔ)

    匈(xiōng) 拾(shí)

9. 鈎(gōu) 梧(wú) 桐(tóng) 鎖(suǒ) 番(fān) 滋(zī) 味(wèi) 崔(cuī) 映(yìng)

10. 拘(jū) 枚(méi) 灣(wān) 峽(xiá)

共計101個生字

生词表（简）

1. 总集 宴会 讲述 风貌 雎鸠 窈窕 淑女 逑 彼 兮 萧 艾

2. 屈原 楚辞 形式 浪漫 基础 放逐 悲愤 求索 奔放 联合 抵抗 命运 歇 尸体 撒 粽子 端午节

3. 乐府 朴素 广泛 亦 军帖 替 征 骏马 暮 唤 赴 欲 阁 裳 皆 吟 郊 慈母

4. 律诗 绝句 言 庐山 瀑布 乃 潜入 锦

5. 莫 樽 烹 倾听 圣贤 寂寞 惟 昔时 恣 沽 酌 裘 尔 愁

6. 格式 苏轼 奴 淘 涛 堆 乔 豪杰 姿

7. 钗 （情）绪 泪痕 山盟 （海誓）

8. 怒 潇潇 啸 激烈 尘 耻 犹 驾 踏 饥 胡虏 匈奴 收拾

9. 钩(gōu) 梧桐(wú tóng) 锁(suǒ) 番(fān) 滋味(zī wèi) 题(tí) 庄(zhuāng) 崔(cuī) 映(yìng)

10. 拘(jū) 韵律(yùn lǜ) 枚(méi) 湾(wān) 海峡(hǎi xiá)

共计109个生词

生詞表（繁）

1. 總集 宴會 講述 風貌 雎鳩 窈窕 淑女 逑 彼 兮 蕭 艾

2. 屈原 楚辭 形式 浪漫 基礎 放逐 悲憤 求索 奔放 聯合 抵抗 命運 歇 尸體 撒 粽子 端午節

3. 樂府 樸素 廣泛 亦 軍帖 替 征 駿馬 暮 喚 赴 欲 閣 裳 皆 吟 郊 慈母

4. 律詩 絕句 言 廬山 瀑布 乃 潛入 錦

5. 莫 樽 烹 傾聽 聖賢 寂寞 惟 昔時 恣 沽 酌 裘 爾 愁

6. 格式 蘇軾 奴 淘 濤 堆 喬 豪傑 姿

7. 釵（情）緒 淚痕 山盟（海誓）

8. 怒 瀟瀟 嘯 激烈 塵 恥 猶 駕 踏 饑 胡虜 匈奴 收拾

9. 鈎(gōu) 梧桐(wú tóng) 鎖(suǒ) 番(fān) 滋味(zī wèi) 題(tí) 莊(zhuāng) 崔(cuī) 映(yìng)

10. 拘(jū) 韻律(yùn lù) 枚(méi) 灣(wān) 海峽(hǎi xiá)

共計109個生詞

新双双中文教材 13
New Chinese Language and Culture Course

中国诗歌欣赏 Appreciation of Chinese Poetry

（第二版）

练习本 单课

[美] 王双双 编著

北京大学出版社

目　录

第一课　　诗经 …………………………………………………… 1

第三课　　乐府 …………………………………………………… 6

第五课　　唐诗（二）…………………………………………… 11

第七课　　宋词（二）…………………………………………… 17

第九课　　古诗词二首 ………………………………………… 22

第一课 诗经

一 写生词

述						讲	述				
彼						宴	会				
兮						风	貌				
萧						雎	鸠				
艾						窈	窕				
总	集					淑	女				

二 每字组二词

电影　集体　礼貌

集 { _____　　貌 { _____　　影 { _____

三 下列汉字是由哪些部分组成的

诗 → □ + □　　　鸠 → □ + □

第一课 诗经

四 选字组词

（影　景）响　　（彼　皮）此　　（编　篇）写

（影　景）色　　（彼　皮）球　　一（扁　篇）

五 给下面的词语加拼音

睢鸠	_____		窈窕	_____

淑女	_____		叔叔	_____

六 将方框中的词句与适当的解释连线

窈窕淑女　　　　　　　　一天没见到，就像隔了三个月

睢鸠　　　　　　　　　　一种水鸟

彼采葛兮　　　　　　　　美丽善良的好姑娘

一日不见，如三月兮　　　那个姑娘采葛去了

七 选择填空

1. 《诗经》是中国第一部_____。

　　A. 历史书　　　　B. 诗歌总集　　　　C. 小说

第一课 诗经

2. 相传《诗经》是_____所编。

  A. 孔子　　　　　　　B. 李白

3. 《诗经》是_____。

  A. 中国京剧的起点　　　B. 中国古代诗歌的起点

4. 《关雎》是一首描写_____的诗。

  A. 两只水鸟　　　　　　B. 青年男女爱情

5. 我们现在用的"一日不见，如隔三秋"出自_____。

  A. 唐诗　　　　　　　　B.《诗经》"一日不见，如三秋兮！"

八　用楷书、隶书、篆书抄写"一日不见，如隔三秋"

一日不见，如隔三秋	楷书	
一日不见，如隔三秋	隶书	
一日不见，如隔三秋（篆书）	篆书	

第一课 诗经

九 诗配画：抄写诗歌《关雎》（带标点）

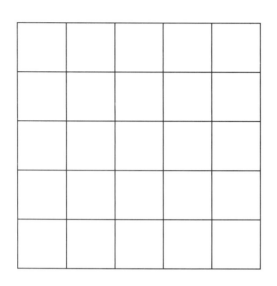

十 抄写诗歌《采葛》一遍（带标题和标点）

十一 造句

例：看电影时大声说话会影响别人。

影响_____

第一课
诗经

十二　自己写一首古体诗，记住句尾加个"兮"字

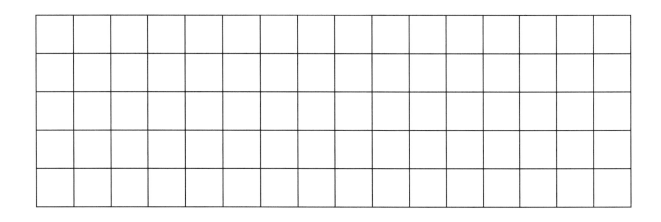

十三　背诵诗歌《关雎》《采葛》

第三课 乐府

一　写生词

亦					
替					
征					
暮					
唤					
赴					
欲					
阁					

裳					
皆					
乐府					
朴素					
广泛					
军帖					
骏马					

二　每字组二词

广场　官府　一伙

府 { _____

伙 { _____

广 { _____

第三课 乐府

三 下列汉字是由哪些部分组成的

府 → ☐ + ☐   欲 → ☐ + ☐

帖 → ☐ + ☐   赴 → ☐ + ☐

四 选字组词

（衣 依）裳   叫（唤 换）

（衣 依）靠   （唤 换）衣服

五 给下面的词语加拼音

唤 _____   可汗 _____

六 将方框中的词句与适当的解释连线

骏马	讲一个姑娘替父从军的故事
乐府	木兰不愿意做官
《木兰辞》	好马
木兰不用尚书郎	是国家专管音乐的一个机构

第三课 乐府

七 选择填空

1. 汉代，乐府从民间收集到的诗歌和乐曲叫_____。

　　A. 楚辞　　　　　　　　　　　　B. 乐府民歌

2. 《木兰辞》是_____。

　　A. 乐府诗　　　B. 楚辞　　　C. 诗经

3. 可汗是_____。

　　A. 古代西北民族对君主的称呼　　　B. 将军

八 将《木兰辞》下列诗句翻译成白话

昨夜见军贴，可汗大点兵。_____

阿爷无大儿，木兰无长兄。_____

愿为市鞍马，从此替爷征。_____

脱我战时袍，著我旧时裳。_____

出门看火伴，火伴皆惊忙。_____

同行十二年，不知木兰是女郎。_____

第三课 乐府

九 抄写《木兰辞》下列诗句,并背诵诗歌前五句

昨夜见军帖,可汗大点兵。军书十二卷,卷卷有爷名。

阿爷无大儿,木兰无长兄,愿为市鞍马,从此替爷征。

选修诗歌《游子吟》

一 写生词

吟					
郊					

慈	母				

二 选择填空

1. 《游子吟》的作者是_____。

　　A. 战国屈原　　　　　B. 唐朝孟郊

第三课 乐府

2. 《游子吟》是描述＿＿＿＿＿＿＿＿＿＿的诗歌。

    A. 伟大的母爱　　　　B. 儿子远游

三　抄写《游子吟》，并背诵

四　做一张卡片给妈妈，上面有你抄写的《游子吟》

（可将作业扫描或拍照发老师）

第五课 唐诗(二)

一 写生词

莫					
樽					
烹					
惟					
恣					
沽					
酌					

裘					
尔					
愁					
倾	听				
圣	贤				
寂	寞				
昔	时				

二 每字组二词

小径 眼镜 圣人 婚宴

镜 {_____

宴 {_____

圣 {_____

径 {_____

第五课 唐诗（二）

三 下列汉字是由哪些部分组成的

樽 → ☐ + ☐   裘 → ☐ + ☐

酌 → ☐ + ☐   愁 → ☐ + ☐

四 选字组词

（樽 尊）敬　　（莫 寞）哭　　（古 沽）酒

金（樽 尊）　　寂（莫 寞）　　（古 沽）代

五 给下面的词语加拼音

尊敬 _____　　　樽 _____

六 将方框中的词语与适当的解释连线

金樽	斟酒，饮酒
钟鼓	精美的酒杯
千金裘	乐器
酌	特别贵重的皮衣

第五课 唐诗（二）

七 选择填空

1. 《将进酒》的作者是_____。

   A. 孟郊　　　　　B. 杜甫　　　　　C. 李白

2. "君不见，黄河之水天上来，奔流到海不复回。"

   比喻_____。

   A. 黄河的源头太高　　　　　　B. 时光飞快过去

3. "君不见，高堂明镜悲白发，朝如青丝暮成雪。"

   比喻_____。

   A. 头发白得太早　　　　　　B. 人生的短暂

4. "人生得意须尽欢，莫使金樽空对月。"

   意思是_____。

   A. 抓紧享受和朋友饮酒笑谈的快乐　　B. 没完地喝酒

5. "天生我材必有用，千金散尽还复来。"

   表达了李白_____的心情。

   A. 自信有能力成大事，不在乎金钱　　B. 花钱大方

第五课 唐诗（二）

八　把意思相同的字词连起来

沽　　烹　　不要　　暮　　昔时

九　把《将进酒》中你喜欢的句子写出来，说说为什么

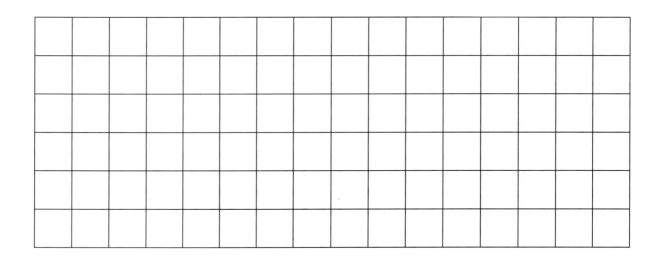

第五课 唐诗（二）

十　书法练习：写出篆书《将进酒》中的前十个字或更多

十一　图中李白像个摇滚歌手喝酒高唱。如果你做某件事失败了，李白诗中哪句话能说出你的心情

_____

_____

第五课 唐诗（二）

十二　下面哪些词"属于"李白？请写在方框、圆圈中

| 淘气 | 自信 | 死板 | 浪漫 | 普通 | 酷（cool） |

| 骄傲 | 天才 | 诗仙 | 寂寞 | 酒中仙 |

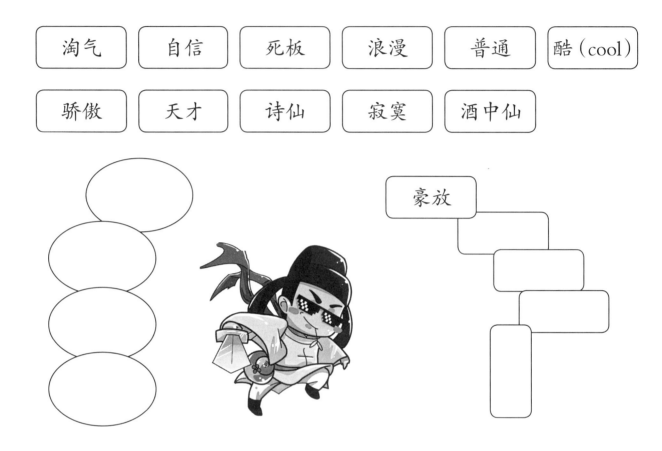

十三　背诵《将进酒》的前八句

第七课 宋词（二）

一 写生词

钗					
情	绪				
泪	痕				

山	盟	海	誓		

二 每字组二词

> 愁绪　泪痕　亭台楼阁　柳叶

绪 { _____
　　 _____ }

阁 { _____
　　 _____ }

柳 { _____
　　 _____ }

泪 { _____
　　 _____ }

三 组新字

金 + 叉 → ☐　　　　金 + 帛 → ☐

门 + 各 → ☐　　　　秋 + 心 → ☐

第七课 宋词（二）

四　选字组词

楼（阁　各）　　（柳　聊）天　　情（绪　续）

（阁　各）人　　（柳　聊）树　　继（绪　续）

五　给下面的词语加拼音

柳树 _____　　聊天 _____

六　猜字谜

"口"进门：　问　　　　"木"进门：_____

"耳"进门：_____　　"心"进门：_____

七　将方框中的词语与适当的解释连线

红酥手　　　　　　　女人细软的手

一怀愁绪　　　　　　离别

离索　　　　　　　　沾湿

浥　　　　　　　　　满心的愁苦

鲛绡　　　　　　　　手帕

第七课 宋词（二）

☆ ---------- ☆ ---------- ☆

八 选择填空

1. 陆游是_____人。

　　A. 南宋　　　　B. 唐朝

2. 陆游的《钗头凤》是_____。

　　A. 诗　　　　　B. 词

3. "春如旧，人空瘦"意思是_____。

　　A. 春天如期而至，可是心上人已十分憔悴

　　B. 春天如期而至，可是来游玩的人少了

4. "桃花落，闲池阁"意思是_____。

　　A. 桃花落了，没有人看桃花了

　　B. 桃花散落，池边楼阁冷冷清清

5. "山盟虽在，锦书难托"意思是_____。

　　A. 山盟海誓在心中，却无法表达

　　B. 山盟海誓还在，但没人送信了

九 选词填空

1. _____酥手，_____滕酒。（红　绿　蓝　黄）

第七课 宋词（二）

2. 满城_____宫墙柳。（春色　秋色）

3. _____恶，欢情薄。（东风　南风　北风）

4. 春如旧，人空_____（胖　瘦）

5. 桃花落，_____池阁（闲　忙）

6. 山盟虽在，_____书难托（信　锦）

十　抄写陆游的《钗头凤》（包括题目、作者、标点）

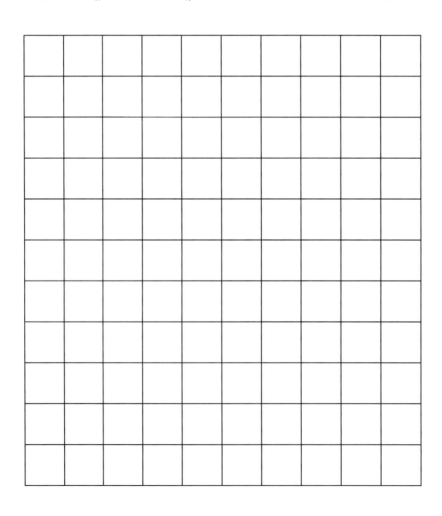

第七课 宋词（二）

十一　写出陆游《钗头凤》中你喜欢的句子

第九课 古诗词二首

一　写生词

钩					
锁					
番					
题					
庄					

崔					
映					
梧	桐				
滋	味				

二　每字组二词

　　　剪不断　锁门　味道　铁钩

锁 { _____ }

味 { _____ }

剪 { _____ }

钩 { _____ }

三　组新字

金 + 勾 → ☐

木 + 同 → ☐

前 + 刀 → ☐

口 + 未 → ☐

第九课 古诗词二首

四　选字组词

（剪　前）面　　（滋　慈）母　　铁（沟　钩）

（剪　前）刀　　（滋　慈）味　　水（沟　钩）

五　读出框中接龙游戏，把不认识的字写在方格中

味
滋味—味道—好味道—香味—甜味—咸味—酸味
酸甜味—苦味—辣味—鲜味—肉味—臭味—烟味
糊味—粤菜味道—川菜味道—鲁菜味道—没味道

六　给下面的词语加拼音

滋味 _____　　　一番 _____

第九课 古诗词二首

七 找出方格中不同的字，写在空格中加拼音再组词

钩	钩	钩	钩
钩	钩	钩	钩
钩	钩	钩	沟

锁	锁	锁	锁
锁	销	锁	锁
锁	锁	锁	锁

滋	滋	滋	滋
滋	慈	滋	滋
滋	滋	滋	滋

☐ 拼音_____   ☐ 拼音_____   ☐ 拼音_____

组词_____   组词_____   组词_____

八 将方框中的词句与适当的解释连线

寂寞　　　　　　　　不知美丽的姑娘哪里去了

人面不知何处去　　　孤独冷清

无言独上西楼　　　　离别之苦

离愁　　　　　　　　独自登上西楼

月如钩　　　　　　　一弯残月

第九课 古诗词二首

九 选择填空

1. 《相见欢》（无言独上西楼）的作者是＿＿＿＿＿＿。

   A. 李白　　　　　　　B. 李煜

2. 李煜是南唐的＿＿＿＿＿＿。

   A. 皇帝　　　　　　　B. 将军

3. "剪不断，理还乱，是离愁"表达了李煜＿＿＿＿＿＿。

   A. 离开国土心中愁苦的滋味

   B. 整理东西越整理越乱

4. "人面桃花相映红"意思是＿＿＿＿＿＿。

   A. 人和桃花都漂亮　　　B. 美丽的姑娘在一树桃花旁多么动人

5. "桃花依旧笑春风"意思是＿＿＿＿＿＿。

   A. 在春风中桃花还是照样盛开　　　B. 桃花喜欢春风

十 在诗中填写正确的字

去年今日＿＿＿＿门中，（此　比）

人面桃花相映＿＿＿＿。（黄　蓝　红）

第九课 古诗词二首

人面不知何_____去，（外　处）

桃花_____旧笑春风。（依　衣）

十一　抄写《相见欢》（无言独上西楼），包括题目、作者、标点

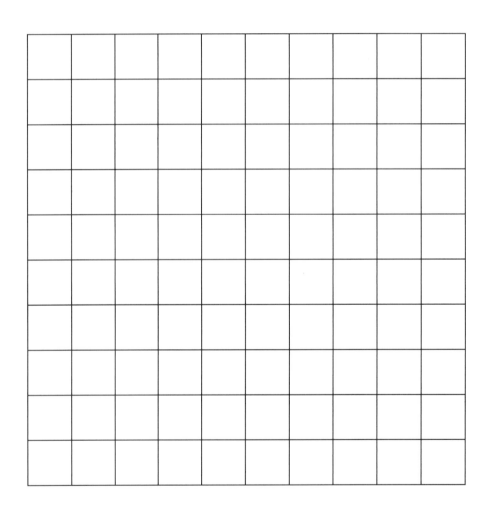

十二　背诵《相见欢》《题都城南庄》

第一课　听写

1.	2.	3.	4.
5.	6.	7.	8.
9.	10.	11.	12.

第三课　听写

1.	2.	3.	4.
5.	6.	7.	8.
9.	10.	11.	12.

第五课　听写

1.	2.	3.	4.
5.	6.	7.	8.
9.	10.	11.	12.

第七课　听写

1.	2.	3.	4.
5.	6.	7.	8.
9.	10.	11.	12.

第九课　听写

1.	2.	3.	4.
5.	6.	7.	8.
9.	10.	11.	12.

1.	2.	3.	4.
5.	6.	7.	8.
9.	10.	11.	12.

1.	2.	3.	4.
5.	6.	7.	8.
9.	10.	11.	12.

1.	2.	3.	4.
5.	6.	7.	8.
9.	10.	11.	12.

第九课　听写

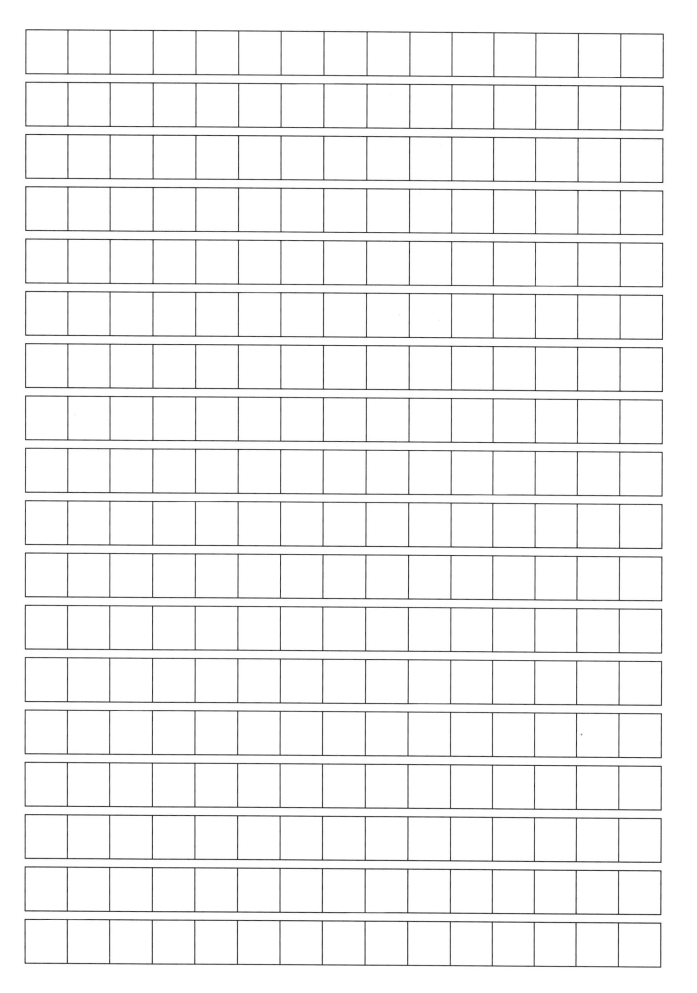

新双双中文教材 13

New Chinese Language and Culture Course

中国诗歌欣赏 Appreciation of Chinese Poetry

（第二版）

练习本 双课

[美] 王双双 编著

北京大学出版社
PEKING UNIVERSITY PRESS

目 录

第二课　屈原与楚辞 ………………………………………………… 1

第四课　唐诗（一）…………………………………………………… 6

第六课　宋词（一）…………………………………………………… 11

第八课　宋词（三）…………………………………………………… 16

第十课　现代诗 ……………………………………………………… 21

第二课 屈原与楚辞

一 写生词

歇					
撒					
屈	原				
楚	辞				
形	式				
浪	漫				
基	础				
放	逐				
悲	愤				

求	索				
奔	放				
联	合				
抵	抗				
命	运				
尸	体				
粽	子				
端	午	节			

二 每字组二词

悲痛　歇一歇　告辞　波浪

辞 { _____ / _____ }

悲 { _____ / _____ }

浪 { _____ / _____ }

歇 { _____ / _____ }

第二课 屈原与楚辞

三 下列汉字是由哪些部分组成的

辞 → ☐ + ☐

础 → ☐ + ☐

屈 → ☐ + ☐

悲 → ☐ + ☐

四 选字组词

（形 开）式　　（歇 喝）水　　浪（漫 慢）

（形 开）始　　（歇 喝）息　　快（漫 慢）

五 给下面的词语加拼音

屈原 _____　　　　端午节 _____

六 将方框中的内容与适当的解释连线

屈原	是中国第一位伟大的诗人
端午节时间	屈原创造的一种新的诗歌形式
楚辞	赛龙舟，吃粽子
端午节活动	在每年的农历五月初五

第二课
屈原与楚辞

七 根据课文选择正确答案

1. 屈原是＿＿＿＿＿＿楚国人。

　　A. 春秋时期　　　　B. 战国时期

2. 屈原的作品中最著名的是＿＿＿＿＿＿。

　　A.《诗经》　　　　B.《离骚》

3. 中国诗歌的源头是由＿＿＿＿＿＿共同构成的。

　　A. 楚辞　　　　　　B.《诗经》与楚辞

4. 为了纪念屈原，端午节的主要活动有＿＿＿＿＿＿。

　　A. 吃饺子　　　B. 舞龙舞狮　　　C. 赛龙舟、吃粽子

八 抄写并背诵屈原名句

路漫漫其修远兮，吾将上下而求索。

第二课
屈原与楚辞

九　将词语与相应的图或文连线

| 吾 | 粽子 | 农历五月初五 |

端午节

十　写出谁是孔子，谁是屈原，并给屈原的衣服涂成蓝色

十一　根据课文选词填空

1. 屈原是战国时期楚国人，是一位伟大的_____。（诗人　猎人）

第二课 屈原与楚辞

2. 他创造了一种新的诗歌形式＿＿＿＿＿。（楚辞　《诗经》）

3. 楚辞的句中、句尾常用"＿＿＿"字表示语气。（啊　兮）

4. 屈原主张联合其他国家共同＿＿＿秦国。（抵抗　欢迎）

5. 楚王不听屈原的话并把屈原＿＿＿。（放逐　放跑）

6. 屈原在放逐的生活中一直关心楚国的＿＿＿。（命运　运气）

7. 屈原看到秦军打败楚国，在＿＿＿＿＿＿投江自杀。

（农历五月初五　春节）

8. 老百姓划船，往江里撒米喂鱼去救＿＿＿。（孔子　屈原）

9. 农历五月初五人们要赛龙舟、吃粽子，过＿＿＿节。（端午　中秋）

十二　画一张"端午节"的图画（可用其他纸画）

提示：端午节、五月初五、屈原、粽子、赛龙舟

十三　口头讲述"屈原和端午节的故事"（2分钟）

第四课 唐诗(一)

一　写生词

言					
律	诗				
绝	句				

庐	山				
瀑	布				

二　每字组二词

法律　几层　语言　楼房

楼 {＿＿＿＿＿＿
　　＿＿＿＿＿＿

律 {＿＿＿＿＿＿
　　＿＿＿＿＿＿

层 {＿＿＿＿＿＿
　　＿＿＿＿＿＿

言 {＿＿＿＿＿＿
　　＿＿＿＿＿＿

三　下列汉字是由哪些部分组成的

庐 → □ + □　　　楼 → □ + □

层 → □ + □

第四课 唐诗（一）

四　选字组词

（绝　色）句　　　（瀑　暴）布　　　（登　瞪）山

红（绝　色）　　　（瀑　暴）雨　　　（登　瞪）眼

五　给下面的词语加拼音

绝句 _____　　　　红色 _____

六　将方框中的词句与适当的解释连线

白日依山尽	想要看得更远
欲穷千里目	傍晚太阳靠着山边慢慢落下
日照香炉生紫烟	阳光照着香炉峰，紫云袅袅
疑是银河落九天	全诗八句，每句五字
五言律诗	就像是九重天上的银河落下来

七　根据课文选择正确答案

1. 《登鹳雀楼》是一首_____。

　A. 五言绝句　　　　B. 五言律诗

第四课 唐诗(一)

2. 《望庐山瀑布》是一首_____。

    A. 五言绝句   B. 七言绝句

八 选词填空

> 李白　王之涣

1. 《登鹳雀楼》的作者是_____。

2. 《望庐山瀑布》的作者是_____。

九 词语解释

1. 依——_____

2. 尽——_____

3. 欲——_____

第四课 唐诗(一)

十　抄写诗歌《登鹳雀楼》《望庐山瀑布》（包括作者）

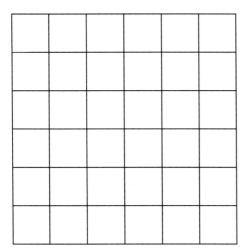
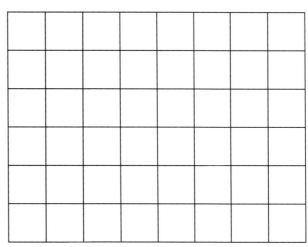

十一　背诵《登鹳雀楼》《望庐山瀑布》

选修 《春夜喜雨》

一　写生词

乃					
锦					

潜	入					

二　选择填空

1.《春夜喜雨》是一首_____。

　　A. 七言绝句　　　B. 五言律诗

第四课 唐诗（一）

2. 《春夜喜雨》的作者是_____。

  A. 李白   B. 王之涣   C. 杜甫

三 将方框中的词句与适当的解释连线

随风潜入夜	田野小路
润物细无声	春雨随风在夜里悄悄落下
野径	静静滋养着万物

四 背诵《春夜喜雨》

第六课
宋词（一）

一　写生词

奴					
淘					
涛					
堆					

姿					
格	式				
苏	轼				
豪	杰				

二　每字组二词

　　　　　　　　　　　　　　　　墙壁　念书　怀里　考卷

念 { _____ 　　　　　　　壁 { _____

怀 { _____ 　　　　　　　卷 { _____

三　选适当的词填空

一（堆）雪　　　　　　　　一堆_____

一堆_____　　　　　　　一堆_____

第六课
宋词（一）

四　组新字

女 + 又 → ☐　　　今 + 心 → ☐

车 + 式 → ☐　　　次 + 女 → ☐

五　给下面的词语加拼音

考卷 _____　　羽扇纶巾 _____

卷起 _____　　堆 _____　　姿 _____

六　把意思相近的词语涂上相同的颜色

赤　　豪杰　　惊涛　　江山

红　　英雄　　国家　　大浪

第六课
宋词（一）

七 将方框中的词语与适当的解释连线

怀古	指周瑜
风流人物	代指强大的敌人
樯橹	这里指英雄人物
周郎	追念古代的事情
故垒	古代军营的墙壁或工事

八 选择填空

1. 《念奴娇·赤壁怀古》的作者是_____。

   A. 李白　　　　B. 苏轼　　　　C. 孟郊

2. 《念奴娇·赤壁怀古》是_____。

   A. 唐诗　　　　B. 宋词　　　　C. 楚辞

3. 苏轼是_____文学家。

   A. 战国时期　　B. 北宋　　　　C. 唐朝

第六课
宋词(一)

4. 《念奴娇·赤壁怀古》中"大江东去"指的是_____。

   A. 长江　　　　B. 黄河

5. "大江东去，浪淘尽，千古风流人物。"

意思是_____

   A. 历史如长江水滚滚东流，千百年来涌现出许多英雄豪杰。

   B. 黄河水滚滚东流，千百年来涌现出了许多名人。

九　找出诗中跟周瑜有关的词语，写在方框中

   大江东去　千古风流人物　豪杰　故国神游

   雄姿英发　周郎　小乔

第六课 宋词(一)

十 抄写《念奴娇·赤壁怀古》（包括题目、作者、标点）

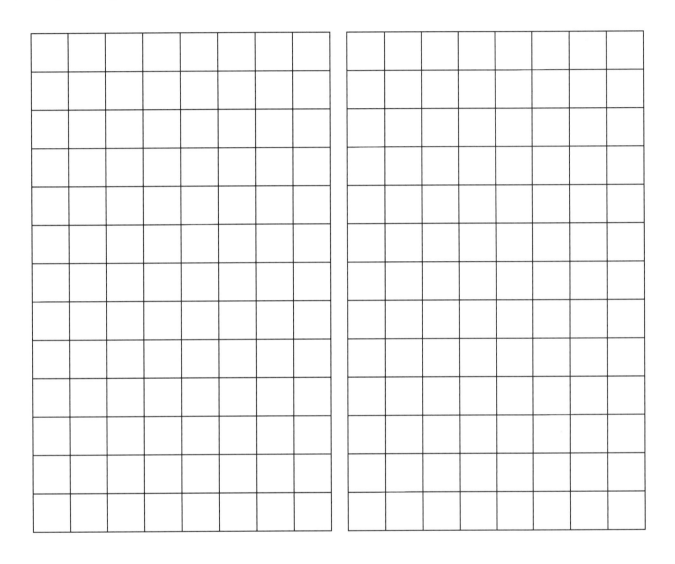

第八课
宋词（三）

一　写生词

怒					
啸					
尘					
耻					
犹					
驾					
踏					

饥					
潇	潇				
激	烈				
胡	虏				
匈	奴				
收	拾				

二　每字组二词　　　　　　　　　　闲话　热烈　念奴娇　驾照

闲 { ____　____ }　　　　烈 { ____　____ }

奴 { ____　____ }　　　　驾 { ____　____ }

第八课
宋词(三)

三　组新字

任 + 几 ⟶ ☐　　　耳 + 止 ⟶ ☐

门 + 木 ⟶ ☐　　　加 + 马 ⟶ ☐

四　选字组词

楼(阁　闲)　　(驾　加)车　　热(列　烈)

(阁　闲)事　　(驾　加)减　　下(列　烈)

五　给下面的词语加拼音

潇潇 _____　　　　啸 _____

六　将方框中的词语与适当的解释连线

胡虏　　　　　　　靠着栏杆

凭栏处　　　　　　外敌,这里指金国人

壮怀激烈　　　　　贺兰山口

贺兰山缺　　　　　壮志在心中激荡

潇潇雨歇　　　　　潇潇的细雨停了

第八课 宋词（三）

七 选择填空

1. 《满江红·写怀》的作者是_____。

   A. 苏轼　　B. 岳飞

2. 岳飞是_____人。

   A. 汉朝　　B. 南宋

3. 《满江红·写怀》表达了岳飞_____。

   A. 要报仇雪恨收回国土的悲壮心情

   B. 已收回国土的快乐心情

4. "仰天长啸"意思是_____。

   A. 抬起头向着长空大喊一声

   B. 低着头大喊一声

5. "莫等闲，白了少年头，空悲切"意思是_____。

   A. 头发白了悲伤

   B. 不能让时光轻易流走，结果一事无成而悲伤

第八课 宋词（三）

八 抄写《满江红·写怀》上阕（包括题目、作者、标点）

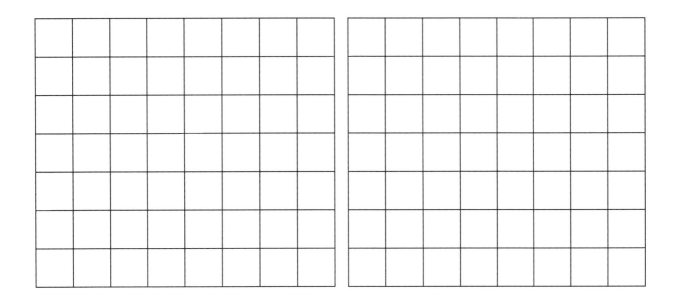

九 读"岳飞抗金的故事"回答问题

　　岳飞是南宋抗金名将。他小时家里很穷，没有钱买纸和笔，就用沙子当纸，用树枝当笔学写字。长大了他又学习武术，武艺高强。之后他带领宋军与金兵作战，多次打败金兵，收回了大片疆土。一次，金兵一万五千人与岳飞作战，人和马都披着铁甲，非常厉害。但岳飞看到了金兵的弱点：马腿上没有铁甲。他让士兵们拿着刀斧，等敌人冲来时，就弯着身子专砍马腿。马受伤倒地，金兵也跌下马来。士兵们勇敢杀敌，宋军大胜。可是宋朝皇帝却想与金国和谈，就下令让岳飞退兵。岳飞内心悲愤，仰天长叹，只好带领军队返回。不想宰相秦桧（huì）硬说岳飞

第八课
宋词（三）

要反皇上，将岳飞和他的儿子岳云杀害了，那时岳飞年仅三十九岁。据说岳飞一生指挥过一百多场战斗，没吃过一次败仗，是名副其实的常胜将军。

选词填空

1. 岳飞是_____的抗金名将。（著名　无名）

2. 岳飞带领宋军打败了金兵的铁甲_____。（骑兵　水兵）

3. 宋朝皇帝不_____岳飞。（了解　信任）

4. 岳飞被杀害了，可是人们_____岳飞。（热烈　热爱）

第十课 现代诗

一 写生词

拘					
枚					
湾					

韵	律				
海	峡				

二 每字组二词

窄小　峡谷　邮局　港湾

邮 { _____
　　 _____

窄 { _____
　　 _____

峡 { _____
　　 _____

湾 { _____
　　 _____

三 在方框中选择适当的词填空

一枚_____　　一番_____

一个_____　　一辆_____

一本_____　　一张_____

第十课 现代诗

四 写出反义词

浅——　　　　　　　　　　窄——

五 选字组词

海（湾　弯）　　邮（票　漂）　　新（娘　狼）

转（湾　弯）　　（票　漂）亮　　灰（娘　狼）

六 读出框中接龙游戏，把不认识的字写在方格中

邮

邮票 — 邮局 — 邮件 — 邮递员 — 邮费 — 邮车

七 给下面的词语加拼音

邮票 _____　　　　汽油 _____

第十课 现代诗

八 找出方格中不同的字,写在空格中加拼音再组词

湾	湾	湾	湾
湾	弯	湾	湾
湾	湾	湾	湾

浅	浅	浅	浅
浅	浅	浅	浅
浅	浅	钱	浅

☐ 拼音_____

组词_____

☐ 拼音_____

组词_____

九 将方框中的词语与适当的名词连线

> 一枚小小的
> 一方矮矮的
> 一张窄窄的
> 一湾浅浅的

坟墓
邮票
海峡
船票

十 选择填空

1.《乡愁》的作者是_____。

    A. 李白   B. 余光中

第十课 现代诗

2. 《乡愁》写出了_____的感情。

    A. 思念朋友   B. 思念故乡和亲人

十一　在《乡愁》的诗句中填写正确的字

1. 乡愁是一枚小小的_____票。（邮　油）

2. 乡愁是一张窄窄的_____票。（般　船）

3. 乡愁是一方矮矮的_____墓。（坟　纹）

4. 乡愁是一湾浅浅的海_____。（侠　峡）

十二　抄写诗歌《乡愁》一遍（包括题目、作者）

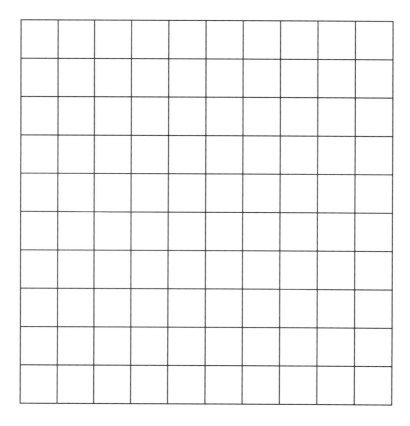

第十课 现代诗

十三　写一首现代诗，描写我们的生活

_____

_____

_____

_____

第二课　听写

1.	2.	3.	4.
5.	6.	7.	8.
9.	10.	11.	12.

第四课　听写

1.	2.	3.	4.
5.	6.	7.	8.
9.	10.	11.	12.

第六课　听写

1.	2.	3.	4.
5.	6.	7.	8.
9.	10.	11.	12.

第八课　听写

1.	2.	3.	4.
5.	6.	7.	8.
9.	10.	11.	12.

第十课　听写

1.	2.	3.	4.
5.	6.	7.	8.
9.	10.	11.	12.

1.	2.	3.	4.
5.	6.	7.	8.
9.	10.	11.	12.

1.	2.	3.	4.
5.	6.	7.	8.
9.	10.	11.	12.

1.	2.	3.	4.
5.	6.	7.	8.
9.	10.	11.	12.

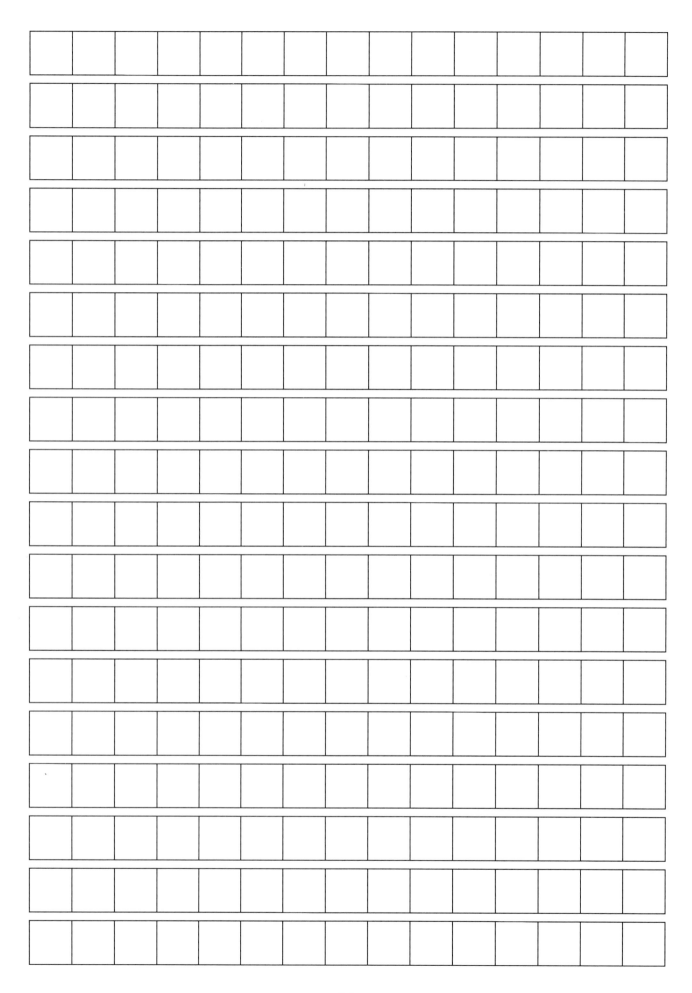